A GUIDE TO FINANCE

For Personal and Professional Life

Siddhartha Mukhopadhyay (born 1969) is a Kolkata-based journalist working in the finance sector for about three decades. After passing ICWA (intermediate) and CA (intermediate), he worked as an investment consultant. Simultaneously, he started writing for newspapers and weeklies in English and Bengali. He went on to become a full-time journalist and worked for the print (including *Ebela* from the ABP group) and electronic media (including ETV News and a news portal). Presently, he is engaged in contributing articles to newspapers and magazines and writing books.

A GUIDE TO FINANCE

For Personal and Professional Life

Siddhartha Mukhopadhyay

First published in 2025 by Hachette India
(Registered name: Hachette Book Publishing India Pvt. Ltd)
www.hachetteindia.com

1

ISBN 978-93-5731-500-5

Hachette Book Publishing India Pvt. Ltd
4th & 5th Floors, Corporate Centre
Plot No. 94, Sector 44, Gurugram – 122003, India

Typeset in Athelas 10/13
by Avishek Bhattacharya

Printed and bound in India
by Thomson Press India Ltd.

IMAGE COPYRIGHT INFORMATION

Folio: *N center/Shutterstock.com*

Chapter title design: *N Universe/Shutterstock.com*

Introduction opener: *GreenTree/Shutterstock.com*

Did You Know: *Aleksandr_Lysenko/Shutterstock.com*

Quick Byte: starline/freepik.com

Section openers

Foundation of Financial Literacy: *PixelSenses/Shutterstock.com*

Personal Finance Essentials: *stockshoppe/Shutterstock.com*

Saving, Investment and Wealth Creation: *jd8/Shutterstock.com*

Business and Financial Health: *Photo by Nataliya Vaitkevich/pexels.com*

Borrowing and Debt Management: *sommart sombutwanitkul/Shutterstock.com*

Financial Risks, Frauds and Protection: *Feng Yu/Shutterstock.com*

Regulation and Grievance Redressal: *iQoncept/Shutterstock.com*

Legacy and Estate Planning: *M21Perfect/Shutterstock.com*

CONTENTS

PREFACE

Good financial behaviour is your saviour! Although relatively new to human civilization, the need for computer literacy has been significantly recognized but the need for financial literacy, on the other hand, has not been discussed to that extent. However, money has been an integral part of human life for ages. And a concrete understanding of all systems that revolve around the concept of money is crucial to living life to one's full potential.

Even to use software smartly, one needs to have financial literacy. Using smartphones for monetary transactions is increasingly becoming common. But, without understanding financial concepts, legitimacy and viability of investment schemes and potential threats arising from digital transfer of money and measures to counter them, one can be easily duped. Falling into debt traps or getting into unnecessary litigation can only be avoided with reasonable financial literacy.

Financial literacy covers a wide range of skills and knowledge which help individuals make informed decisions about their money. Even in non-financial jobs the basic understanding of financial terms is needed too.

Moreover, I have noticed that a lack of financial literacy not only affects individuals but also society as a whole. One clear example is the 2008 global financial crisis, which was partially triggered by widespread misunderstanding of mortgage products and irresponsible borrowing. In India, financial literacy has seen some improvement in recent years, but significant gaps remain. The lack of basic financial knowledge leads to poor financial decisions including investment blunders.

In this book, I have tried to discuss the basic ideas of finance that the common man needs to know in his day-to-day life. In addition to finance, relevant business and commerce topics are also discussed. The book has a holistic approach to financial literacy instead of just being an investment guide or a book on personal finance. This book will boost your professional life as well, even if you do not work in the financial sector.

And now, I should acknowledge my journalist friend Nilanjan Dey – without his support, this work would not have seen light of the day. I should acknowledge my indebtedness to the editorial team of my publisher Hachette India. Last but not the least, I convey my thanks to Anirban Sarkar who took the initiative to publish this book.

– Siddhartha Mukhopadhyay

INTRODUCTION

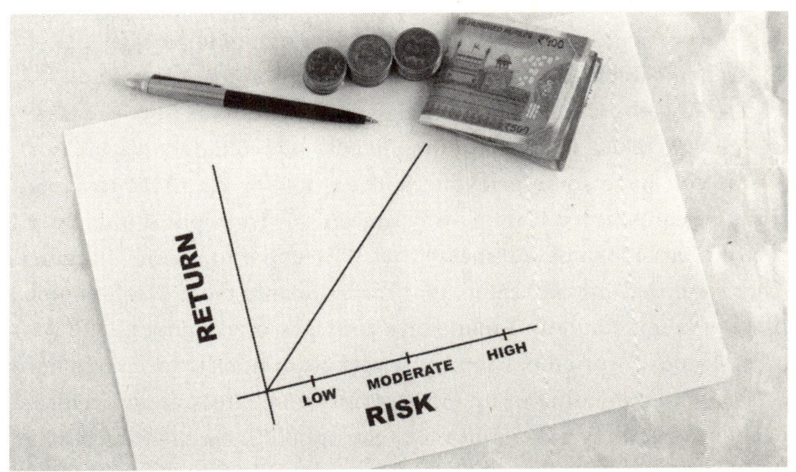

FINANCIAL LITERACY AS A SKILL FOR LIFE AND WORK

WHY FINANCIAL LITERACY MATTERS TODAY

A person who is financially aware is less likely to fall victim to financial fraud and mis-selling, which are rapidly rising in India and across the world. From basic banking to digital payments, understanding money-related decisions helps individuals to make informed and safe choices. Financial literacy includes knowing how to manage debt, track expenses, save for retirement and create personal budget skills that are just as relevant at the workplace as they are at home.

Over the past few decades, the way we use money has changed significantly. Older generations relied mostly on cash. Today we have access to credit cards, online wallets, Unified Payments Interface (UPI) applications (apps) and electronic transfers. This shift makes financial understanding essential. But financial literacy goes even deeper. For instance:

- How many of us know the legal aspects of making a will?
- What is the importance of mentioning a nominee?
- What is the risk factor in savings and investment?
- How to take a loan for funding needs but avoid debt traps?
- If you have some grievances, then how to get them resolved?

Thus we can see that it is not only the various concepts of finance but also the basic idea of commerce that is essential to financial literacy. These are real-life situations that many people face. Also, financial literacy is not limited to managing your personal budget. It plays a critical role at work too. Even professionals in non-finance roles need a basic understanding of financial terms to be effective and relevant in their jobs. In a non-finance job, you should have the basic idea of business and commerce too as a greater aspect of finance.

Understanding basic business terms like topline, bottom line and profit and loss (P&L) reports are essential for strategic planning, managing teams, allocating resources wisely and evaluating performance. Without this knowledge, it becomes difficult to measure success or plan for the future. Financial literacy is not just about knowing how to save or invest, it is also about making smarter decisions in all areas of life.

SCOPE OF FINANCIAL LITERACY

Financial literacy covers a wide range of skills and knowledge that help individuals make informed decisions about their money. Some of the core areas include managing and repaying debt, creating a household budget and evaluating the advantages and risks of different credit and investment options. These skills often require at least a basic understanding of key financial concepts such as compound interest and the time value of money.

In today's financial landscape, it is also important to understand topics like health insurance, student loans, mortgages and self-directed investment accounts. Financial literacy should cover both short-term and long-term planning, including how current financial decisions can impact future tax liabilities. It also involves knowing the most suitable investment avenues for retirement planning, managing everyday expenses, preparing long-term budgets and having a basic grasp of business finance.

WHERE DO WE STAND NOW?

Lack of financial literacy does not just affect individuals. It can impact entire economies. One clear example is the 2008 global financial crisis, which was triggered in part by widespread misunderstanding of mortgage products and irresponsible borrowing. Millions faced foreclosures and the ripple effects destabilized economies across the world. This crisis showed how poor financial decisions by individuals can lead to massive economic consequences.

According to a 2019 survey conducted by the National Centre for Financial Education (NCFE) on behalf of the Securities and Exchange Board of India (SEBI), only 27 per cent of Indians were found to be financially literate. This low level of financial awareness extended further when gender was considered, with even fewer women having basic financial knowledge. You can check the details here: https://ncfe.org.in/nflis/.

In contrast, countries in Europe, the US and Australia demonstrate financial literacy rates between 55 per cent and 75 per cent. This comparison underscores the substantial ground India needs to cover in enhancing financial literacy among its citizens.

UNDERSTANDING BASIC FINANCIAL TERMS

Money is a recognized medium of exchange. Simply put, we need money to satisfy our needs and wants.

In economic terms, a **need** is something essential for survival, such as food, clothing and shelter. A **want** is something we desire to improve our comfort or enjoyment, like a luxury car, a big house or dining at an expensive restaurant.

Currency means the coins and notes used in a country's economy. Each country has its own currency. For instance, India uses the rupee, the US uses the dollar and the UK uses the pound.

A **bank** is a financial institution that holds the money of account holders or depositors. The bank uses this money to provide loans to individuals and businesses, charging interest on those loans while also paying interest to depositors.

An **account** is a financial record held by a bank for a customer. It is identified by a unique account number and can be of various types such as savings account, current account or Fixed Deposit (FD).

Income is the money a person or organization receives in return for providing goods, services or allowing the use of their assets.

- Ingots of silver, with only three dots as a mark, probably represent the earliest form of coinage on the Indian subcontinent (in circulation as early as 600 BCE).
- Cowries were used as legal tender in the Bengal kingdom of Lakhnauti during the reign of Ghiyasuddin Bahadur Shah I (r. 1322–24 CE).

Expense refers to the money spent on regular needs such as rent, utility bills, groceries and transportation.

Savings is the portion of income that remains after all expenses are paid. It reflects the amount set aside for future use.

An **investment** is an asset purchased with the aim of generating income or increasing in value over time.

A **loan** is a specific amount of money borrowed from a bank or financial institution or from a money lender under agreed conditions. It must be repaid along with interest within a certain time period.

FOUNDATION OF FINANCIAL LITERACY

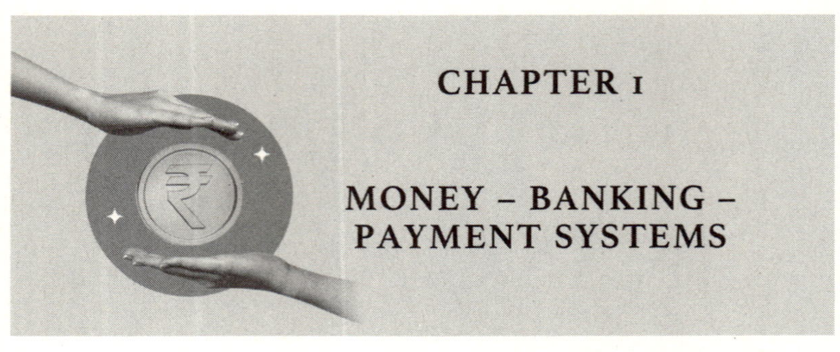

CHAPTER 1

MONEY – BANKING – PAYMENT SYSTEMS

We cannot ignore money, as it is such an important aspect of our lives. But what is the meaning of money? Most of us usually think of currency notes, such as ₹500 or ₹100, as money. It helps us to buy various goods and services that we require in our daily lives. Money also helps us understand the value of a product and decide whether it is priced high or low. Today money exists mainly in the form of notes that we can easily carry in our wallets or deposit safely in banks. The more money we have, the greater our ability to buy what we want. In this way, money plays an important role as a store of value. While money cannot buy emotions, this does not reduce its significance; money does matter.

The Reserve Bank of India (RBI) has the sole right to issue banknotes in India, as per Section 22 of the RBI Act. According to Section 25, the design, form and material of these notes are determined by the central government after reviewing recommendations from the central board of the RBI. However, there is one exception for the issue of ₹1 note. Among all denominations, the ₹1 note is issued by the Ministry of Finance (MoF) and it bears the signature of the finance secretary, while other notes bear the signature of the governor of the RBI. Despite being legal tender, ₹1 notes are seldom used in circulation due to their minimal value.

AUTONOMY OF RESERVE BANK OF INDIA

In India, the central bank is the RBI. The Reserve Bank's primary responsibility is to regulate the issuance of currency notes and the management of reserves to maintain monetary stability in India and optimize the country's monetary and credit systems. This is achieved by establishing a contemporary monetary policy framework that is capable of addressing the challenges of an increasingly intricate economy, ensuring price stability while maintaining the goal of growth. Under the Reserve Bank of India Act and its various amendments, extensive powers have been granted to the RBI. Although the word autonomous does not appear in the Act, the principle of central bank autonomy has become widely accepted over time. It is now regarded as a fundamental and enduring aspect of its functioning.

While the RBI is technically owned by the Ministry of Finance (MoF) and its board is appointed by the government, the RBI operates with a degree of autonomy. The MoF can issue directions to the RBI in the public interest. Still the RBI has its mandate to regulate the banking system and currency, which is responsible for monetary policy. There may be instances where the MoF and the RBI hold differing views on specific policies, leading to discussions and negotiations. However, ultimately, the RBI has the authority to make its decisions. The extent to which the RBI governor is accountable to the central government remains a debatable issue. In practice, disagreements between the MoF and the RBI governor can, sometimes, hit serious levels.

FISCAL POLICY AND MONETARY POLICY

Everyone should have a basic understanding of who is responsible for controlling money and managing the economy of our country. The RBI and the central government play key roles in this area. In this context, two important terms to understand are monetary policy and fiscal policy. The monetary policy formulated and implemented by the RBI is primarily focussed on regulating money supply, interest and inflation rates. The RBI uses instruments such as the repo rate and open market operations to influence liquidity in the financial system and control borrowing costs.

The repo rate is the interest rate at which the RBI lends funds to commercial banks. Alterations in the repo rate, therefore, influence borrowing expenses and liquidity within the economy. Conversely, the reverse repo rate is its antithesis. Consequently, it is the interest rate at which India's central bank secures loans from commercial banks. Open market operations entail the purchase and sale of government securities to manage money supply and interest rates.

For example, in response to rising inflation, the RBI can increase the repo rate to make borrowing more expensive and curb excessive spending. On the other hand, in times of economic downturn, the RBI can lower interest rates to encourage borrowing and stimulate investment. The RBI conducts the Monetary Policy Committee (MPC) meeting every two months, marking six meetings per financial year.

The MPC is a six-member committee responsible for determining the policy rate (repo rate) in India. This is used to manage inflation and achieve the government's inflation target. The MPC is a statutory body established under the RBI Act of 1934. It is headed by the RBI governor and includes a deputy governor in charge of monetary policy, one officer nominated by the RBI's central board and three members appointed by the central government.

On the other hand, fiscal policy refers to government decisions related to taxation, public spending and budget allocations. The government uses fiscal policy to manage overall demand, support economic growth and address social and economic challenges. For instance, during the

COVID-19 pandemic, the Indian government increased spending on healthcare, infrastructure and social welfare programmes. Additionally, tax reductions and stimulus packages were implemented to encourage consumer spending, which in turn helped revive economic activity. It is managed by the MoF.

BANK AND PAYMENT SYSTEM

When you were young, you probably had a piggy bank. A piggy bank, in which you keep cash or coins, is a form of savings. When you finally open it, it gives you a wonderful reward in the form of a lot of money that would have accumulated by then – a lot for a child, may not be for an adult. This way you also get an idea of savings as well as the concept of a bank and how they work in real life.

Banks: What They Are and Why We Need Them

Let us understand the concept of banking with the help of an example. Consider a situation where a person (lender) lends some money to another person (receiver) without any receipt or a similar type of evidence. After a while, the lender demands his money back, but the receiver fails to comply. The lender cannot approach the police or file a lawsuit against the receiver because of the lack of evidence.

Consider a different scenario in which a specialized institution assumes the role of a lender. This institution maintains proper documentation and offers loans at a predetermined interest rate. Along with the loan, it clearly outlines the terms of repayment, including the time frame within which the amount must be repaid. If the borrower fails to repay the loan within the stipulated period, the institution may impose penalties or take further action as per the agreement.

This important institutional role is performed by banks. A bank is a financial system licenced by the governing authority to lend money to people in the form of loans and receive money from them as savings and deposits. However, it works according to strict rules and also serves many more functions that are important to individuals and businesses.

In short, a bank acts as a 'vault' for the safekeeping of money. And when people need more money than their savings – to buy or build a house or buy a car or to start a business, to name a few such situations – banks also grant loans to people who have deposited money with them.

Banks play an essential role in the development of our nation:

- Banks help in economic development by providing loans to farmers, service members, business people and organizations.
- Banks provide people and businesses with the opportunity to convert their savings into investments.
- Banks raise the standard of living by providing loans for consumer goods, homes, automobiles, etc.
- Banks identify our country's backward regions and help in their economic and social development by providing them adequate funds at reasonable interest rates.

Origins of Banking

The origins of banking can be traced back to ancient civilisations, particularly in the temples and palaces of Babylonia as early as 2000 BCE, where deposits were accepted and loans were issued. The ancient Greeks later developed a rudimentary banking system, including money lending and the use of written records for transactions.

Modern banking in India began with the establishment of the Bank of Hindustan in 1770, although it ceased operations by 1832. The foundation of institutional banking was further laid with the establishment of the Bank of Calcutta in 1806, which was later renamed the Bank of Bengal. It was followed by the Bank of Bombay in 1840 and the Bank of Madras in 1843. These three presidency banks were merged in 1921 to form the Imperial Bank of India.

After Independence, the Government of India (GoI) and the RBI nationalized the Imperial Bank in 1955, renaming it State Bank of India (SBI). Today SBI remains the oldest surviving and largest public sector bank in India. Alongside public sector banks, India also has a robust presence of private and foreign banks contributing to the financial system.

Types of Banks

Banks are of different types and can be categorized on the basis of their ownership and services they offer:

Central Bank: The RBI performs the duties of a central bank in India. It has to manage the currency system of the country to maintain a sufficient provision of authentic currency notes. The RBI has a diverse range of functions in its capacity as a central bank. Other than managing the currency, the RBI serves as a banker for the government and executes the country's monetary policies. So, these are its main functions:

- Acting as the key issuer of currency notes
- Managing the foreign currency reserves of the country
- Controlling money supply in the economy
- Acting as a custodian for the reserve money
- Checking and monitoring all the activities of the commercial banks of a country

Commercial Banks: Commercial banks are financial institutions that accept deposits from the public and provide credit for consumption and investment. They offer various financial services such as savings and current accounts, fixed deposits, personal and business loans, debit and credit cards and digital banking. These banks serve as a bridge between depositors and borrowers, playing a key role in the economic development of the country.

Commercial banks in India are broadly classified into the following categories:

- **Public Sector Banks:** These are majority-owned by GoI. They have a large network across the country and are trusted by a wide section of the population. Examples include SBI, Bank of Baroda (BoB), Punjab National Bank (PNB), UCO Bank etc.

- **Private Sector Banks:** These are owned and operated by private individuals or corporations. They are known for efficient services and modern banking facilities. Popular examples include HDFC Bank, ICICI Bank, Axis Bank and Kotak Mahindra Bank.
- **Foreign Banks:** These are international banks that operate in India through branches. They bring global banking practices and cater to high-end customers and corporates. Examples include Hongkong and Shanghai Banking Corporation (HSBC), Standard Chartered Bank (SCB) and American Express Banking Corporation (AEBC).
- **Regional Rural Banks (RRBs):** These were established to provide banking facilities to rural and semi-urban areas. They mainly serve farmers, small entrepreneurs and the rural people. RRBs are jointly owned by the central government, state government and sponsoring public sector banks.

Investment Banks: An investment bank serves as a financial brokerage firm, facilitating intricate and sizable financial dealings. Typically, investment banks assist startup firms during their Initial Public Offering (IPO) and during mergers with competing firms. Investment banks also offer brokerage and advisory services to large institutional clientele – for example, fund managers of pension funds.

Cooperative Banks: The cooperative banking system aims to generate a culture of saving and investment, especially in rural parts of the country. They provide funding to people to buy livestock or invest in agriculture, including dairy farming. They also provide personal finance and help in self-employment.

Specialized Banks: These banks are established to provide financial support to specific sectors such as foreign trade and industrial development. Notable examples include the Export-Import Bank of India (EXIM Bank), the Small Industries Development Bank of India

(SIDBI) and the National Bank for Agriculture and Rural Development (NABARD). These institutions offer targeted credit facilities; policy support and developmental initiatives tailored to their respective sectors.

Small Finance Banks (SFB): These have emerged as a new category of banks in India that cater primarily to the financially unserved and under-served sections of society. These banks have been set up with a strategic objective of promoting financial inclusion by offering basic banking services to the unbanked and under-banked population and making formal credit available to this segment.

- Payments Banks: It is like any other bank, but operates on a smaller scale without taking on credit risk. These are banks that can't offer loans or issue credit cards. These banks can accept demand deposits of up to ₹1 lakh. They also do money transfers for you and assist in mobile payments, remittances, purchases and other banking services. They can issue ATM or debit cards and run internet banking and third-party transfers.

OPENING A BANK ACCOUNT

A bank account can be opened in the name of an individual, either singly or jointly with a family member, by submitting the following documents:

- Passport size photographs
- Address proof
- Identity proof
- Opening amount

Once the account is opened, the bank provides to the account holder an account number and cheque book to operate the account and use an ATM card from time to time. Now banks also provide account holders with access to net banking and mobile banking.

TYPES OF BANK ACCOUNTS

Savings Account: A savings account is designed to encourage the habit of saving among individuals. It offers the flexibility to deposit any amount at any time, making it a convenient option for daily banking needs. This type of account is especially popular among students, salaried individuals and senior citizens. It also earns nominal interest, depending on the duration for which the funds are kept in the account.

Demand deposits are bank account balances that a customer can withdraw at any time without prior notice. They offer high liquidity and are widely used for daily transactions. For example, your savings account or current account in a bank is a demand deposit. You can withdraw money through ATM, cheque or online transfer whenever you need it. These deposits are called 'demand' because the bank must release the funds on demand of the account holder.

Current Account: Generally, business owners open current accounts to handle frequent and high-volume transactions, including unlimited

The Punjab National Bank Ltd, the first private bank wholly owned and run by Indians, opened in 1895.

The first regional rural banks (RRB) in India were opened in Moradabad and Gorakhpur in Uttar Pradesh, Bhiwani in Haryana, Jaipur in Rajasthan and Malda in West Bengal on 2 October 1975.

The Chartered Bank, established in 1853 in Madras, was the earliest foreign bank in India. In 1969, it merged with the Standard Bank in London, UK and was incorporated as the Standard Chartered Bank. This is the first foreign bank on the Indian soil.

The National Housing Bank (NHB), a subsidiary of the Reserve Bank of India, was established on 9 July 1988. This is the first bank for housing development in India.

The Bank of India was the first Indian bank to open a branch outside India, in London, UK, in 1946 and also the first to open a branch in Paris, France, in 1974.

The Greater Bombay Cooperative Bank Ltd, India's first cooperative bank, was registered on 5 November 1952 under the Bombay State Cooperative Act, with 50 members and an initial capital of ₹21,000.

deposits and withdrawals. Unlike savings accounts, current accounts do not earn interest. However, banks may provide an overdraft facility, allowing account holders to withdraw more than their available balance to meet urgent business needs. In such cases, banks charge interest on the overdrawn amount.

Fixed Deposit (FD): An FD, also known as a term deposit or time deposit, involves depositing a lump sum amount for a fixed period at a predetermined rate of interest. At the end of the tenure, the account

- ATMs allow customers to withdraw cash, check balances and perform basic banking anytime.
- ATM in India was introduced by The Hong Kong and Shanghai Banking Corporation (HSBC), at its head office in Mumbai (then Bombay) in 1987.
- Debit cards are linked to bank accounts and deduct money directly during purchases or withdrawals.
- Credit cards allow users to borrow up to a set limit, to be repaid later with or without interest.
- The first credit card in India was introduced by the Central Bank of India in 1980. It was called the Central Card.

holder receives the principal amount along with the accrued interest. The key benefit of a fixed deposit is that it offers a significantly higher rate of interest compared to a savings account.

Recurring Deposit (RD): This offers higher interest rates than a savings account. Here you deposit a fixed amount at a fixed interval. For example, you deposit ₹1,000 per month over twenty-four months. At the end of twenty-four months, you get ₹24,000, plus interest.

Is It Mandatory?

No, current account is not compulsory for business. But at the same time, think about savings accounts; there are a number of restrictions on banking service facilities. And keep in your mind the relatively high volume of transaction for the business, so instead of saving, a current account is a more convenient option to run a business smoothly.

For Micro, Small and Medium Enterprises (MSME), a separate current account will begin to give you a clearer picture of the profits and losses in your business. Having a separate bank account for the business can help in better management of finances and can also help in availing various government schemes and benefits. For large business houses too, a current account is not legally mandatory. However, given the high volume and frequency of transactions involved in business operations, the limited features of a savings account are often insufficient. As a result, maintaining a current account becomes practically essential for efficient financial management.

Accrued interest is the amount of interest that builds up over time and will be received (or paid) later. For example, in an FD, your money earns interest every day, even if you receive the total only at the end of the term.

Whenever you open these types of accounts, it is important to mention a nominee. In the absence of nomination, it could be expensive and time consuming for the legal heirs of the deceased accountholder to get the money. It is better to open those accounts in joint name with another person instead of a single name to avoid unnecessary harassment in some odd situation.

CHEQUE – AN INSTRUMENT OF EXCHANGE

A cheque is a type of bill of exchange in which one party instructs a bank to transfer a specified amount of money to another party's bank account. It is a negotiable instrument governed by the Negotiable Instruments Act, 1881. Cheques have long been a popular means of transferring money, particularly before the rise of digital banking. Although many people now prefer online transfers, cheques still play an important role in banking.

How Does a Cheque Work?

Let us understand with a simple example:

Suppose you have ₹25,000 in your account at ABC Bank and you wish to pay ₹5,000 to Mr A. Basu by cheque. The process is as follows:

1. You write a cheque of ₹5,000 to Mr A. Basu using your ABC Bank cheque book.
2. Mr Basu deposits the cheque in his bank, say XYZ Bank.
3. XYZ Bank sends the cheque for clearing to ABC Bank.
4. ABC Bank verifies the cheque and transfers ₹5,000 to XYZ Bank.
5. XYZ Bank credits ₹5,000 to Mr Basu's account.
6. ₹5,000 is debited from your account at ABC Bank.

Key Elements of a Cheque

A cheque typically contains

- the name and signature of the person issuing the cheque,

- the name of the person or entity receiving the payment,
- date on which the cheque is issued or becomes valid.

To enhance the security of cheque payments, the RBI introduced the Positive Pay System (PPS). This system helps prevent cheque-related fraud by requiring the person issuing the cheque to confirm important details with the bank before the cheque is processed. Under PPS, you must provide the following details to your bank before the cheque is presented for clearance:

- Cheque number
- Date
- Amount
- Name of the beneficiary

These details can be submitted through a bank branch, internet banking, mobile banking or SMS. PPS is mandatory for cheques above a certain value, depending on the bank's policy.

Cheque dishonour

A cheque is dishonoured when the bank is unable to process it, usually due to reasons such as insufficient funds, mismatched signatures, overwriting, incorrect account number or invalid dates. If a cheque is dishonoured due to insufficient funds, the bank returns it along with a return memo. The drawer may also face legal consequences, including prosecution under the Negotiable Instruments Act, which can result in fines and/or imprisonment.

Banking Facilities for Elderly, Sick or Incapacitated Persons

Banks in India provide special provisions to assist senior citizens, bedridden individuals and physically challenged persons in conducting financial transactions when they are unable to visit the branch or operate their accounts independently.

1. Withdrawal Using Thumb Impression

- If a person is unwell, elderly or physically disabled, they

On 4 October 2025, the RBI introduced a new system. Now the cheque clearing system is much faster. In the new system, a cheque is cleared within hours instead of one or two working days.

In the new system, cheques are not processed in fixed batches. After scanning, banks send the cheques to the clearing house continuously in the banking hours (10 am to 4 pm). So each cheque is settled in near real-time, in just a few hours.

can authorize withdrawals using a thumb impression instead of a signature.

- **Requirement:**
- The thumb impression must be witnessed by two independent persons known to the bank (e.g., neighbours, relatives or bank officials).
- The witnesses must sign and provide their identification details (Aadhaar, PAN, etc.).

2. Alternative Method for Those Unable to Provide Thumb Impression

- If a person cannot even provide a thumb impression and is unable to visit the bank, they can still authorize transactions by:
- Making a mark (e.g., 'X') on the cheque/withdrawal form.
- Two independent witnesses must verify the mark and confirm the account holder's identity.

3. Authorizing a Representative for Withdrawals

- If the account holder is completely incapacitated, the bank may allow a trusted representative (family member/caretaker) to withdraw money on their behalf.
- **Process:**

  The bank will record the representative's details (name, relationship, ID proof).
- The representative must submit the cheque/withdrawal form with the account holder's mark/thumb impression.
- Two independent witnesses must verify the transaction.

4. Additional Support for Incapacitated Customers

- **Home Banking Services:** Some banks offer doorstep banking for elderly/sick customers (e.g., cheque pick-up, cash delivery).

RESERVE BANK OF INDIA (RBI)

Established in 1935 and nationalized in 1949. The RBI is India's central bank. The bank issues currency in India and also destroys notes and coins that are not fit for use. Apart from the issuance of currency, the RBI performs various other essential functions that impact the development of the Indian economy in a significant way:

- The RBI is the monetary management authority of India that regulates interest rates and maintains prices to keep inflation in check.
- The RBI is the banker and the debt manager to the GoI.
- It is also the banker to the other banks in India.
- It is the body for financial regulation and supervision in India.
- The RBI is responsible for foreign exchange management and foreign exchange reserve management.
- The RBI also supervises and regulates market operations, payment and settlement systems and research and data dissemination.

NATIONAL PAYMENTS CORPORATION OF INDIA (NPCI)

It was founded in December 2008, National Payments Corporation of India

The RBI acts as the banker and debt manager to the GoI by maintaining its accounts, managing receipts and payments and providing temporary funding through Ways and Means Advances. It also oversees the issuance and repayment of government securities like bonds and treasury bills, conducts auctions to raise funds from the market and advises the government on borrowing and debt management strategies.

(NPCI) is incorporated under section 25 of Companies Acts 1956(now it is a Section 8 company under the Indian Companies Act, 2013) and has been set up by the Reserve Bank of India and Indian Banks' Association. The Certificate of Commencement of Business was issued in April 2009. Its products and services include retail payment services like Unified Payments Interface (UPI) and cheque truncation (electronic image of the cheque is transmitted to the drawee bank by NPCI along with relevant other information). It also acts as the national automated clearing house.

UNIFIED PAYMENTS INTERFACE (UPI)

UPI is a mobile-based payment system developed by NPCI that allows users to link multiple bank accounts in a single app. It enables quick fund transfers and merchant payments without needing to enter bank details or Indian Financial System Code (IFSC) for every transaction. (A detailed discussion on UPI appears in Chapter 2.)

RUPAY

With the evolution of payment systems, RuPay has made a significant impact on the retail payments ecosystem in India. A product of NPCI, RuPay is the first-of-its-kind domestic card payment network, exclusively developed for the Indian market. The name RuPay is derived from the words rupee and payment.

In recent years, RuPay has introduced various card variants catering to different segments of society. In addition to government scheme cards, RuPay offers classic, platinum and select variants designed to serve both the masses and affluent customers. These cards come with a range of privileges and benefits including international acceptance, domestic and international airport lounge access, complimentary personal accidental death and permanent total disability insurance cover, attractive merchant offers, cashback schemes and health and wellness benefits, thereby appealing to a wide range of users.

Currently, RuPay cards are issued by numerous banks, including public sector banks, private sector banks, regional rural banks and cooperative banks. Its ten core promoter banks are SBI, PNB, Canara Bank, BoB, Union Bank of India, Bank of India, ICICI Bank, HDFC Bank, Citibank National Association and HSBC.

LOCKER

Safe deposit locker are provided by banks to its their customers who use them to keep their important and valuable items such as documents and jewellery etc safe.

Such lockers are specially designed and are kept in specially built strong rooms of the bank branches. Lockers are in different sizes and bank charges locker rent as per their size.

Customers should keep in their mind that they are not allowed to store any illicit items (cash, weapons, drugs etc) or use the locker for unlawful purposes.

It is the responsibility of the bank to compensate the customer in case of any loss in locker due to fault of the bank. But in such situation bank is liable to pay 100 times of the annual locker rent. So, if annual rent of the locker is Rs 500 then maximum compensation is ₹5,00,000.

MINIMUM AVERAGE BALANCE

Considering the position and condition of customers various banks offer zero-balance savings account facilities. Generally, salary accounts of the employees of an organization are zero balance account.

Other than those customers have to maintain minimum average balance which varies with location (urban, semi urban, rural) of the branch of the bank. Minimum average balance of an account is the lowest average amount of money that a customer has to maintain in his bank account to avoid non maintenance charges or penalties. It is calculated on the basis of the daily closing balance.

The minimum average balance is decided by the particular bank. So, different banks have different amounts. The RBI has recently clarified that it cannot regulate the minimum average balance of any bank, so such decision are left to individual banks.

Generally private banks are seen imposing penalties for non-maintenance of minimum average balance, while public sectors banks waive such penalties for financial inclusion.

CHAPTER 2

DIGITAL INDIA – TRANSFORMING INDIA INTO A DIGITAL ECONOMY

Digital India is one of the most ambitious initiatives launched by the GoI to transform the country into a digitally empowered society and knowledge-driven economy. Launched on 1 July 2015, this programme aims to make technology accessible to every citizen, especially in rural and remote areas. It focuses on enhancing internet connectivity, promoting digital literacy, encouraging the use of online services and supporting digital entrepreneurship.

The vision of Digital India is to create an inclusive digital ecosystem where government services are available to all through online platforms. It aims to bridge the digital divide by offering affordable internet, promoting mobile connectivity and integrating technology into everyday life. By promoting cashless transactions, digital payments, e-governance and startup innovation, Digital India is not only transforming how people interact with technology but also contributing to the development of a stronger, more transparent and more efficient economy.
This programme focuses on the following:

DIGITAL INFRASTRUCTURE AS A CORE UTILITY TO EVERY CITIZEN

- Providing high-speed internet in all rural and urban areas (e.g., BharatNet).

- Offering a unique digital identity to every individual through Aadhaar, which are unique numbers issued by the Unique Identification Authority of India (UIDAI).
- Ensuring mobile connectivity and access to digital resources for all.
- Creating public internet access points, such as Common Service Centres (CSCs).
- Building cloud-based services and national digital platforms.

GOVERNANCE AND SERVICES ON DEMAND

- Delivering government services online (e-governance) in real time.
- Ensuring easy access to documents via platforms like DigiLocker.
- Promoting cashless and paperless transactions through UPI and digital payments.
- Integrating services via apps like Unified Mobile Application for New-age Governance (UMANG) and portals like Government e-Marketplace (GeM), e-Hospital and e-Courts.
- Enabling direct benefit transfer (DBT) using Aadhaar-linked bank accounts.

DIGITAL EMPOWERMENT OF CITIZENS

- Promoting digital literacy, especially in rural areas (e.g., Pradhan Mantri Gramin Digital Saksharta Abhiyan or PMGDISHA).
- Making digital content and services available in Indian languages.
- Encouraging citizen engagement through apps like MyGov and grievance portals.
- Ensuring accessibility through affordable devices, public training and open platforms.

EXPANDED FOCUS AREAS (2020–2025 AND BEYOND):

- FinTech and Financial Inclusion: Promoting UPI, Bharat Interface for Money (BHIM), RuPay, Jan Dhan accounts and digital wallets.

- Artificial Intelligence (AI): Launching the IndiaAI Mission, AI centres of excellence and Bhashini (language translation tool).
- Startups and Innovation: Supporting digital startups, especially in tier-2 and tier-3 cities.
- Cybersecurity and Data Protection: Enforcing the Digital Personal Data Protection Act, 2023 and increasing cyber awareness.
- Electronics and Semiconductor Manufacturing: Boosting domestic manufacturing through the India Semiconductor Mission (ISM).
- Digital Education and Healthcare: Expanding online learning (SWAYAM, DIKSHA), virtual labs, telemedicine and e-health services.

KEY DIGITAL INDIA INITIATIVES

To turn this vision into reality, the GoI has launched several initiatives under the Digital India umbrella. These key initiatives are designed to make digital services accessible, inclusive and efficient for every Indian citizen. Here are some of the most important ones:

Common Service Centres (CSCs) – September 2006

CSCs are local access points that provide essential digital services in rural and semi-urban areas. They offer services such as bill payments, Aadhaar enrolment, insurance, banking and support for government schemes. Managed by trained Village-Level Entrepreneurs (VLEs), CSCs aim to empower communities through technology. The initiative began in 2006 and expanded with the launch of Digital India in 2015.

Aadhaar Enabled Payment System (AePS) – January 2011

AePS is a digital payment system that allows individuals to conduct basic banking transactions using their Aadhaar number and biometric authentication. It enables cash withdrawals, checking account balance and money transfers without the need for a debit card or smartphone. This system is handy in rural areas with limited banking infrastructure, promoting financial inclusion for individuals who lack literacy or access to digital devices.

BharatNet – October 2011

BharatNet is a key project aimed at providing high-speed broadband to all gram panchayats in India. It helps bridge the digital divide by offering reliable internet access to rural areas. With better connectivity, citizens can access online education, healthcare, financial services and government schemes. BharatNet forms the backbone of the Digital India mission, promoting digital inclusion. It was initially known as the National Optical Fibre Network (NOFN).

MyGov – July 2014

MyGov is a platform launched by the GoI to enhance public participation in policymaking. It enables citizens to share ideas, provide suggestions, participate in surveys and discussions by encouraging two-way communication. MyGov promotes a more transparent and responsive approach to governance.

eBiz Portal – January 2015

The eBiz Portal, developed by the GoI, streamlines government-to-business (G2B) interactions by providing a single online platform for businesses to apply for licences, permits and registrations, as well as file taxes, eliminating the need to visit multiple offices. By consolidating various departmental services, eBiz reduces paperwork, saves time and fosters a more efficient business environment, supporting the vision of Digital India with transparent and effective service delivery.

DigiLocker – July 2015

DigiLocker is a secure, cloud-based platform from the GoI that enables citizens to store, access and share important documents, such as PAN cards, Aadhaar, driving licences and educational certificates in digital form. It eliminates the need for physical copies and allows for quick verification in official procedures, promoting paperless governance and easy access to records. Its adoption is growing among various institutions.

Unified Payments Interface (UPI) – April 2016

UPI is a real-time digital payment system developed by the NPCI that enables users to transfer money instantly between bank accounts using a mobile phone. It supports multiple banks and works 24/7, making cashless transactions fast, simple and secure.

Unified Payments Interface (UPI) has revolutionized digital payments in India and continues to evolve with new features that enhance convenience and safety. One recent development is UPI Lite, which allows small-value transactions (up to ₹1,000) without needing a PIN or even internet access, making it ideal for quick, everyday purchases.

UPI is also expanding globally through partnerships, enabling Indian users to make payments in countries like Singapore, United Arab Emirates and France. Another key innovation is Tap & Pay, which uses NFC technology to allow contactless UPI payments through mobile phones. Additionally, users can now link RuPay credit cards to UPI apps, making it possible to pay merchants using a credit line instead of a bank balance.

To address growing concerns about digital fraud, UPI platforms are introducing enhanced security features, such as real-time alerts, blocking options and easier fraud reporting mechanisms. These improvements make UPI more accessible, flexible and secure for a broad range of users.

Note: Near Field Communication (NFC) is a short-range wireless technology that allows two devices to communicate when they are very close, usually within a few centimetres. It is commonly used for contactless payments, such as tap-and-pay transactions using smartphones or cards.

(See also UPI in Chapter 3)

Government e-Marketplace (GeM) – August 2016

GeM is an online platform that enables government departments and public sector units to purchase goods and services directly from registered vendors. It enhances transparency, eliminates intermediaries and ensures fair pricing by providing a unified and efficient procurement system. GeM also supports small and medium-sized enterprises by providing them with access to government buyers.

Employees' Provident Fund Organization (EPFO) Web Portal – December 2016

The EPFO web portal is an online platform that enables employees to easily manage their Provident Fund (PF) accounts. Through this portal, users can check their PF balance, download their e-passbook, update their details and track the status of their claims without needing to visit the EPFO office. It significantly reduces paperwork, speeds up processes and brings transparency to PF-related services.

Bharat Interface for Money (BHIM) App – December 2016

BHIM is a mobile payment application developed by the NPCI to promote fast and secure digital transactions using the UPI. The app allows users to send and receive money directly from their bank accounts using just a mobile number or UPI ID. BHIM is easy to use, supports multiple Indian languages and does not require an internet connection for basic services, making it ideal for users in both urban and rural areas.

Pradhan Mantri Gramin Digital Saksharta Abhiyan (PMGDISHA) – February 2017

It is a nationwide digital literacy campaign aimed at making at least one person per rural household digitally literate. Under this programme, individuals are trained to use computers, smartphones, the internet, digital banking and online services. It helps bridge the digital divide by empowering rural citizens with the skills needed to participate in the digital world.

SWAYAM and DIKSHA – July & September 2017

These are government-supported e-learning platforms designed to provide free, high-quality education to students, teachers and professionals. SWAYAM offers online courses for school and college students, while DIKSHA focuses on teacher training and classroom content in multiple Indian languages to promote inclusive and flexible learning nationwide.

Unified Mobile Application for New-age Governance (UMANG) – November 2017

UMANG is a mobile application that provides citizens with access to over 2,000 central, state and local government services through a single platform. It helps users to book Liquefied Petroleum Gas (LPG) cylinders, check pension details, access health records, apply for scholarships and much more. It simplifies public service delivery by promoting convenience, transparency and digital empowerment in various Indian languages.

e-Hospital and e-Sanjeevani – July 2015 & April 2020

Digital healthcare initiatives called e-Hospital and e-Sanjeevani provide online access to medical services. Through e-Hospital, patients can book appointments, view lab reports and register at hospitals without having to stand in long queues. e-Sanjeevani enables online doctor consultations, especially in rural areas, through video-based telemedicine. e-Hospital launched in 2015; E-Sanjeevani launched in 2019, with expansion during the COVID-19 pandemic.

Open Network for Digital Commerce (ONDC) – April 2022

It is a government-backed initiative that aims to create an open and inclusive digital marketplace where small businesses, retailers and service providers can sell their products online. Unlike traditional e-commerce platforms controlled by private companies, ONDC enables sellers and buyers to connect freely through a shared network. This helps promote fair competition, increases market access for local businesses and supports digital growth in tier-2 and tier-3 cities.

DIGITAL BANKING: BANKING AT YOUR FINGERTIPS

Digital banking refers to accessing banking services online or through mobile devices, without the need to visit a bank branch. It enables users to check account balances, transfer funds, pay bills, apply for loans and manage their finances at any time and from anywhere. With the rise of smartphones, apps and secure payment systems, banking has become faster, easier and more convenient for everyone.

These are the services offered by digital banking:

Account Management

- View account balance and transaction history
- Download bank statements
- Update personal details (address, mobile number, etc.)

Fund Transfers

- Transfer money using National Electronic Funds Transfer (NEFT), Real Time Gross Settlement (RTGS), Immediate Payment Service (IMPS) or UPI
- Send and receive money instantly through mobile apps

Bill Payments and Recharges

- Pay utility bills (electricity, water, gas)
- Recharge mobile phones, Direct-to-Home (DTH) and data packs

Online Shopping and Merchant Payments

- Make payments directly from bank accounts via UPI or debit cards
- Scan QR codes to pay in shops and markets

Loan and Credit Services

- Apply for personal, home or vehicle loans
- Check loan eligibility and EMIs
- Access credit card services

Investment and Insurance

- Open FD or RD

- Invest in mutual funds or government bonds
- Buy insurance policies (health, life, motor)

Customer Support and Chatbots

- Raise service requests or complaints
- Use chatbots or live chat for help

ATM and Branch Locator Services

- Locate nearby ATMs or bank branches
- Schedule appointments with bank officials (if needed)

Safety Tips for Digital Banking

1. Use Strong Passwords: Use strong passwords that combine letters, numbers and symbols. Avoid sharing personal details, such as your name, date of birth or common words, to keep your digital banking accounts safe from unauthorized access.
2. Enable Two-Factor Authentication (2FA): Use one-time passwords (OTPs) or biometric verification for added security.
3. Avoid Using Public Wi-Fi: Always use secure internet connections when accessing your bank accounts online.
4. Keep Your Devices Secure: Protect your devices by installing antivirus software, enabling automatic updates and setting a screen lock. These steps help secure your digital banking activities from malware, unauthorized access and potential cyber threats.
5. Beware of Phishing Scams: Do not click on unknown links or respond to suspicious emails, SMS messages or calls claiming to be from your bank.
6. Never Share Sensitive Information: Never share your PIN, password, OTP or CVV with anyone, not even bank staff, to protect your banking security.
7. Log Out After Every Session: Always log out of mobile or online banking apps after use.
8. Check Bank Statements Regularly: Regularly review your bank transactions to quickly identify any unauthorized activity and

report it to your bank for immediate action.

9. Download Official Apps Only: Use banking apps only from trusted sources such as the Google Play Store or the Apple App Store to ensure safety and authenticity.
10. Report Suspicious Activity Immediately: Contact your bank's customer care if you notice any unusual activity or receive fake calls/messages.

UNDERSTANDING DIGITAL PAYMENTS

Digital payments refer to financial transactions conducted electronically. Whether it is transferring money to a friend, paying a utility bill, shopping online or scanning a QR code at a local shop, digital payments

Card Verification Value (CVV) is a 3-digit (on Visa, Mastercard, RuPay) or 4-digit (on American Express) security code printed on your debit or credit card.

It is used to verify that the person making an online or card-not-present transaction has the physical card in hand. CVV helps prevent unauthorized use of your card during digital transactions and adds an extra layer of security.

have made everyday banking faster, easier and more convenient. People across India, including those in rural areas, can now send and receive money instantly from the comfort of their own homes, thanks to the rise of smartphones and secure payment platforms.

Advantages of Digital Payments

1. Convenience: Digital payments can be made any time and from anywhere using a smartphone, computer or even a basic mobile device.

2. Speed: Transactions are processed instantly, whether you're transferring money, paying bills or shopping online.
3. Security: Most digital payment systems use encryption, PINs, OTPs and biometric verification to protect user information and prevent fraud.
4. Transparency: Every transaction is recorded, making it easier to track spending, manage budgets and avoid errors.
5. Promotes a Cashless Economy: Reduces the need to carry physical cash, lowering the risks of theft, loss and counterfeit currency.
6. Supports Financial Inclusion: Enables people in rural and remote areas to access financial services without needing to visit a bank.
7. Eco-Friendly: The reduced use of paper receipts, cheques and cash helps mitigate the environmental impact of financial transactions.
8. Boosts Government Initiatives: Helps in delivering subsidies and welfare benefits directly to citizens through digital platforms, reducing delays and corruption.
9. Discourages Black Money: Every transaction is recorded electronically, making it harder to hide income or conduct undeclared transactions. When more people use digital modes, it becomes easier for authorities to monitor income and ensure proper tax reporting.

Modes of Digital Payments

S.No.	Mode of Payments	Descriptions	Usage
1	UPI	Instant money transfer between bank accounts using a mobile phone and UPI ID	Google Pay, PhonePe, Paytm

S.No.	Mode of Payments	Descriptions	Usage
2	**Mobile Wallet**	Stores money digitally for easy payments and recharges.	Paytm Wallet, Amazon Pay
3	**Internet Banking (Net Banking)**	Online access to banking services like fund transfer, bill payment, etc	Bank websites (SBI, HDFC, ICICI)
4	**Debit and Credit Cards**	Plastic cards used for online and offline purchases and ATM withdrawals	Visa, RuPay, Mastercard
5	**QR Code Payments**	Scan-and-pay system using mobile apps and QR codes	BHIM, Google Pay, PhonePe
6	**AePS**	Biometric-based banking using Aadhaar and fingerprint authentication	Micro-ATM transactions in villages
7	**Point of Sale (PoS) Terminals**	Swipe machines used in shops to accept card payments	Card readers in retail stores
8	***USSD Banking (99#)**	Banking through basic phones using USSD codes without internet	Dial *99# for mobile banking services
9	**NEFT**	Batch-based bank-to-bank money transfer during working hours	Net banking portals

S.No.	Mode of Payments	Descriptions	Usage
10	RTGS	Real-time high-value fund transfer (two lakh rupees and above)	Used by businesses and banks
11	IMPS	24/7 instant money transfer through mobile or internet banking	Bank Apps, ATMs

Types of Banking Cards

S.No.	Card Type	Key Features	Usage
1.	Debit Card	PIN-based, no debt risk	Spend from savings account
2.	Credit Card	Rewards, EMI options	Borrow money (Repay later)
3.	Prepaid Card	No bank account needed	Pre-loaded money
4.	RuPay Card	Low-cost, Govt. schemes	India's domestic card
5.	Contactless Card	Tap-and-pay (NFC)	Faster transactions

S.No.	Card Type	Key Features	Usage
6.	Virtual Cards	Digital-only card with a unique card number	subscription payments
7.	Co-branded Cards	Exclusive benefits tied to the partner brand, issued by bank	Earn rewards, cashback or loyalty points

How Card Payments Work: The Key Players

1. **Acquirer Bank:** This is the merchant's bank, which enables businesses to accept card payments. They provide PoS machines where customers swipe, dip or tap their cards.
2. **Issuer Bank:** The bank that issues debit, credit or prepaid cards to customers.
3. **Payment Gateway:** A secure bridge between online merchants and banks. It encrypts transaction details, ensuring safe digital payments (e.g., on websites or apps).
4. **Payment Aggregator:** A service that allows businesses to accept multiple payment methods (UPI, cards, wallets) without needing a separate merchant account. Examples include Razorpay, PhonePe and Google Pay.

Staying Safe with Card Payments

While cards are convenient, security is crucial:

1. Never share your PIN, CVV or card details with anyone.
2. Cover the keypad while entering your PIN at ATMs.
3. Use credit cards wisely – pay dues on time to avoid debt.
4. Report lost/stolen cards immediately to block transactions.
5. Enable transaction alerts for real-time monitoring.

Where Can You Use Cards?

1. **PoS Machines:** Found in stores for card swipes/dips/taps.
2. **Mobile PoS (mPoS):** A smartphone-based card reader (e.g., swipe machines).
3. **Soft PoS (Tap-on-Phone):** Turns an NFC-enabled phone into a card reader, no extra hardware needed.
4. **E-commerce Payments:** Online shopping using card details or saved payment methods.
5. **ATMs: For cash withdrawals, balance checks and more.**
    - On-site ATMs – Located inside bank branches.
    - Off-site ATMs – Stand-alone machines located in malls, gas stations and other public places.
    - White Label ATMs – Operated by non-banking entities (e.g., Tata Indicash).
    - Brown Label ATMs – Outsourced to third-party providers but branded by banks.
6. **Cash Deposit Machines (CDMs):** Allow cash deposits without visiting a bank teller. Some even recycle cash for withdrawals.

CHAPTER 3

EXPLORING DIGITAL PAYMENT MODES – CLICKS TO FINGERPRINTS

The digital payments landscape in India has evolved significantly, offering multiple secure and convenient methods for financial transactions. This chapter introduces three key modes of digital payments: internet banking, biometric-based payments and mobile-based banking. Each section explains how these systems work, their advantages and the security features that protect users.

INTERNET BANKING

Internet banking, also known as online banking, enables customers to conduct financial transactions via a bank's website or app, using a smartphone, tablet or computer. It eliminates the need for physical cheques and allows seamless fund transfers, bill payments and account management.

Key fund transfer methods, some of which you may already know:

National Electronic Funds Transfer (NEFT)

- A nationwide RBI-operated system for electronic fund transfers.
- Transactions are processed in half-hourly batches (48 batches per day).
- Requires the beneficiary's account number, IFSC and name.
- No minimum transfer limit; for non-account holders, the maximum for cash-based transactions is ₹50,000.

Real-Time Gross Settlement (RTGS)

- Designed for high-value transactions with a minimum amount of

₹2 lakhs and no upper limit.

- Funds are transferred in real time and settled individually, making the process fast and irreversible.
- Available 24/7, including holidays.

Immediate Payment Service (IMPS)

- Facilitates instant interbank transfers at any time through mobile banking, internet banking or ATMs.
- Maximum limit of ₹5 lakh per transaction (may vary by bank).
- Offers low transaction fees and immediate settlement.

Biometric-Based Banking

Biometric-based banking uses Aadhaar to authenticate users and facilitate secure transactions, especially in rural and underserved areas.

Unique Identification Authority of India (UIDAI)

UIDAI was established to issue Aadhaar, a 12-digit unique identity number to Indian residents. It enables secure and reliable verification, helping prevent fraud and eliminate duplicate identities.

- Aadhaar Enabled Payment System (AePS) *(see Chapter 2)*
- BHIM Aadhaar Pay *(see later in this chapter)*

The UIDAI manages the world's largest biometric identification system, having issued over 1.3 billion Aadhaar numbers to Indian residents. It ensures layered security through multi-factor authentication methods such as fingerprint, iris scan, OTP and face recognition. To enhance privacy, UIDAI offers offline Aadhaar verification through a QR code printed on the Aadhaar card, allowing identity proof without disclosing full Aadhaar details or biometrics.

Aadhaar, introduced as a voluntary identity system, has now become mandatory for several essential services under legal provisions. It is required for opening bank accounts, obtaining mobile SIM cards and accessing government subsidies and welfare benefits such as LPG, pensions, ration distribution and schemes like PM-KISAN. The

Supreme Court of India, in its 2018 judgment, upheld the constitutional validity of Aadhaar while clarifying that it can only be made compulsory when backed by law. Accordingly, the Aadhaar Act, 2016, along with amendments to other laws like the Prevention of Money Laundering Act, 2002 and the Indian Telegraph Act, 1885, provides the legal basis for its mandatory use in specific sectors. However, private companies are not permitted to demand Aadhaar unless specifically authorized by legislation.

It is not mandatory to provide details to open a bank account, unless you wish to receive any benefit or subsidy under any scheme notified under section 7 of the Aadhaar (Targeted Delivery of Financial and Other subsidies, Benefits and Services) Act, 2016 (18 of 2016).

The authority also introduced the Virtual ID (VID), a temporary 16-digit number that can be used in place of the Aadhaar number to protect user privacy. Additionally, UIDAI offers resident-centric features such as the mAadhaar app, biometric locking and unlocking and the ability to lock/unlock Aadhaar for added user control and security.

MOBILE-BASED BANKING

Mobile-based banking refers to performing financial transactions through a bank's mobile app using a smartphone. This convenient and secure method has become increasingly popular due to rising smartphone usage and internet connectivity.

Services via Mobile Banking

- Fund transfers (NEFT, RTGS, IMPS, UPI)
- Bill payments, recharges
- Fixed deposit/loan management
- Card blocking, cheque book requests

Safety Measures *(See chapter 2)*

Unified Payments Interface (UPI) *(See Chapter 2)*

Mobile Wallets *(See later in this chapter)*

Unstructured Supplementary Service Data (USSD) *(See Chapter 2)*

Other Payment Systems

India's digital payment ecosystem includes several systems beyond internet and mobile banking. These platforms are designed to simplify specific types of transactions for both individuals and institutions.

National Automated Clearing House (NACH)

- A bulk payment system operated by NPCI.
- Facilitates automatic transfer of funds for bulk payments.
- Used for paying salaries, pensions, dividends, subsidies and more.
- Enables recurring collections like EMIs, insurance premiums, utility bills, etc.
- Reduces manual effort and ensures timely settlements.
- Beneficial for both businesses and government departments.

Bharat Bill Payment System (BBPS)

- A centralized bill payment platform that offers bill payment services.
- Covers multiple utility bills such as **electricity, water, gas, DTH, telecom, broadband** and others.
- Provides **anywhere, anytime access** through bank branches, ATMs, online banking, mobile apps and agent outlets.
- Operated by **NPCI** and regulated by the **RBI.**
- Ensures **secure, transparent and error-free** transactions.

How It Works:

1. Access: Customers visit a BBPS-enabled banking app, website, payment app or retail outlet.
2. Select Category: Choose the bill type (e.g., electricity, DTH).
3. Fetch Bill: Enter details (mobile number, customer ID) to view the bill amount and due date.
4. Payment: Select a preferred mode (UPI, net banking, card, wallet).
5. Confirmation: Upon successful payment, customers receive an instant SMS/receipt with a 'Be-Assured' mark. A robust grievance redressal system ensures quick resolution for any issues.

Fast Electronic Toll Collection (FASTag)

- FASTag is affixed to the vehicle's windscreen and linked to a prepaid wallet or bank account which operates under the NETC programme.

- Enables automatic toll deduction at highway toll plazas without stopping.
- Reduces waiting time, fuel usage and traffic congestion.
- Accepted across all national highways and many state highways.
- Made mandatory by the GoI for all vehicles.
- Promotes digital, contactless toll payments.

How It Works:

1. Registration: Users obtain a FASTag from toll plazas, fuel stations or banks.
2. Linking Account: Tags can be linked to savings, current or prepaid accounts.
3. Automatic Deduction: Sensors at toll plazas deduct fees seamlessly

The National Electronic Toll Collection (NETC) system by NPCI has helped reduce toll plaza wait times by over 50%, saving more than 3.4 billion litres of fuel annually, equivalent to cutting 8.7 million tonnes of carbon emissions. It makes NETC not just a time-saver, but also an environmentally friendly innovation.

MICRO ATMS AND MOBILE-BASED BANKING: EXPANDING FINANCIAL ACCESS

Micro ATMs are handheld devices that enable banking services like cash withdrawals and balance enquiries in remote areas using Aadhaar authentication. Mobile-based banking allows users to access and manage their bank accounts through mobile apps or USSD, making financial services more inclusive and accessible, especially in rural regions.

Micro ATMs: Banking at Your Doorstep

In remote areas where traditional ATMs are unavailable, micro-ATMs serve as portable banking solutions operated by authorized banking correspondents (Bank Mitras). These handheld devices enable basic transactions using Aadhaar-based biometric authentication (fingerprint/iris scan), eliminating the need for physical cards or PINs.

Key Features of Micro ATMs:

- Financial Inclusion: Bridges the gap for rural populations with limited bank access.
- Low-Cost Solution: Far more affordable than conventional ATMs.
- Regional Language Support: Enhances usability in diverse linguistic regions.
- Transactions Supported:
- ■ Cash withdrawals & deposits
- ■ Balance enquiries
- ■ Fund transfers (Aadhaar-to-Aadhaar)
- ■ Mini statements

BHIM Aadhaar Pay: Biometric Payments for Merchants

A merchant-focused system that enables cashless payments through Aadhaar-based biometric authentication. It works by verifying the customer's identity using their Aadhaar number and fingerprint to process transactions directly from their linked bank account.

Let's see how it works:

1. Merchant Requirements:
- ■ Android smartphone with BHIM Aadhaar Pay app
- ■ Certified biometric scanner (connected via USB to PoS/micro-ATM)
2. Customer Requirements:
- ■ Aadhaar-linked bank account
3. Transaction Process:

- Merchant enters customer's Aadhaar number, selects bank and inputs amount.
- Customer authenticates via fingerprint/iris scan.
- Payment is processed instantly.

Merchant Onboarding Steps:

1. Download the app from Google Play Store.
2. Register using Aadhaar number and biometrics.
3. Link a bank account for crediting payments.
4. Accept terms and conditions.

Mobile Banking: Your Bank in Your Pocket

Mobile banking empowers users to manage finances via smartphones or tablets, offering 24/7 access without branch visits.

Registration and Activation

1. Three Registration Methods:

- Net Banking: Use existing customer ID and password.
- Debit Card: Enter card number, expiry date and ATM PIN.
- OTP-Based: Verify via SMS OTP sent to registered mobile number.

2. Set Mobile PIN (MPIN): A 4-6-digit code for secure app access.

Services Available via Mobile Banking Apps

Category	Services
Account Management	Check balance, view statements, update profile, locate ATMs/branches.
Transactions	NEFT/RTGS/IMPS transfers, UPI payments, QR code scans, standing instructions.
Card Services	Block/unblock cards, generate PINs, modify limits.
Loans & Investments	Apply for loans (personal, home, gold), invest in stocks/MFs, open FDs.

Category	Services
Bill Payments	Utilities (electricity, water), credit cards, insurance, FASTag recharges.
Lifestyle	Book flights/trains, buy gift cards, donate to charities.

SECURE MOBILE BANKING PRACTICES AND DIGITAL PAYMENT METHODS

To ensure safe mobile banking, follow these security measures:

1. Device Protection

- Set a strong password/PIN to lock your smartphone/tablet.
- Install reputable antivirus software to prevent malware attacks.
- Keep the operating system and apps updated with the latest security patches.

2. Data Security

- Never save banking details (card numbers, CVV, MPIN) on your device.
- Disable auto-fill for login credentials to prevent unauthorized access.
- Delete SMS/email transaction alerts regularly to avoid data leaks.

3. Safe Usage Practices

- Avoid public Wi-Fi for banking, use mobile data or secure networks.
- Log out immediately after completing transactions.
- Use only official bank apps, avoid third-party or fake apps.

4. Fraud Prevention

- Never share OTPs, UPI PINs or MPINs with anyone.
- Register for SMS alerts to monitor account activity in real time.

Unified Payments Interface (UPI)

UPI, as you already know, is a real-time payment system developed by NPCI, enabling seamless fund transfers via a single mobile app. Just a summing up here.

Key Features :

- Single App for Multiple Banks: Link several accounts to one UPI app.
- Virtual Payment Address (VPA): Send/receive money using IDs like name@bank.
- Instant Transfers: Uses IMPS for 24/7 transactions.
- QR Code Payments: Scan merchant QR codes for quick checkouts.

How to Use UPI :

1. Download a UPI app (e.g., BHIM, Google Pay, PhonePe).
2. Register with your linked mobile number and bank account.
3. Create a VPA (e.g., yourname@upi).
4. Set a UPI PIN (using debit card details).
5. Transact via: UPI ID/VPA, QR codes or mobile number (if registered with UPI)

Cost: Free for users (data charges may apply).

BHIM App: Simplified UPI Payments

Developed by NPCI, BHIM offers secure UPI transactions.

Features *(See Chapter 2)*

Steps to Use BHIM :

1. Download the app from Google Play Store/Apple App Store.
2. Select language and permit necessary access.
3. Link your bank account and set a UPI PIN.
4. Send money by entering:

- Recipient's UPI ID
- QR code scan
- Account/IFSC details

QR Code Payments

A contactless method to pay via UPI apps:

1. Scan the merchant's QR code.

2. Verify amount and merchant name.
3. Enter UPI PIN to confirm.
4. Receive instant SMS/app confirmation.

Mobile Wallets

Digital wallets (e.g., Paytm, Google Pay, PhonePe) store money for cashless payments.

Benefits :

- No need for cash/cards, pay via QR codes or app transfers.
- Instant utility bill payments (electricity, DTH, etc.).
- Rewards & cashbacks on transactions.

How It Works

1. Add money via debit/credit cards or bank transfers.
2. Pay merchants via: QR codes, wallet balance, linked cards.

PERSONAL FINANCE ESSENTIALS

CHAPTER 4

CONCEPT OF INCOME AND SALARY

Income refers to the money earned by individuals or businesses in exchange for labour, services, investments or assets. Its classification depends on the context, whether for taxation, accounting or economic analysis. For tax purposes, income is categorized under specific heads to determine tax liability, while in financial accounting, it includes revenue from business operations. Economically, income encompasses wages, dividends, interest and other earnings. Recognizing these distinctions is crucial for financial planning and regulatory compliance.

HEADS OF INCOME (AS PER INCOME TAX ACT, 1961)

The Income Tax Act, 1961, classifies income into five primary categories:

1. Income from Salary

Salary refers to the fixed compensation an employee receives from an employer in exchange for services. It includes basic pay, allowances such as House Rent Allowance (HRA), Transport Allowance (TA), bonuses and other benefits. Taxable salary is calculated after accounting for exemptions like house rent allowance, leave travel allowance and deductions such as PF contributions. The salary slip details all these components, helping employees understand their earnings and tax implications.

2. Income from House Property

It includes rental earnings from residential or commercial properties. For self-occupied properties, the taxpayer may be eligible for certain benefits. Now, what about properties that are neither self-occupied nor rented? Under the Indian Income Tax Act, 1961, if you own more than two self-acquired property and those are not rented out, only two properties can be treated as self-occupied and exempt from tax from rental income. The remaining property/properties, even if lying vacant, is/are deemed to be let out and the notional rent (estimated market rent) for that/those is taxable under *Income from House Property*.

Deductions such as municipal taxes and home loan interest under section 24 help reduce the taxable income.

The government may identify vacant properties through various means, e.g., electricity and water usage data, municipal records or property inspection reports. Low or no utility usage can be a red flag for vacancy. In some cases, housing societies or neighbours may also report prolonged vacancy.

3. Income from Business or Profession

Profits from trade, commerce, manufacturing or professional services fall under this category. Business income is calculated as revenue minus allowable expenses such as operational costs and depreciation. Professionals like doctors, lawyers and freelancers report their earnings under this head.

4. Income from Capital Gains

Profits from selling capital assets (e.g., property, stocks, jewellery, etc) are classified as:

- Short-term capital gains (STCG): Assets held for a short duration (varies by asset type).

- Long-term capital gains (LTCG): Assets held beyond a specified period, taxed at concessional rates.

STCG refer to the profits earned from the sale of capital assets held for a short duration. The specific holding period depends on the type of asset:

- Listed equity shares and equity-oriented mutual funds: Held for less than 12 months
- Immovable property (land or building): Held for less than 24 months
- Other assets (like debt funds, jewellery, etc.): Held for less than 36 months

STCG is usually taxed at a higher rate than long-term capital gains. For example, STCG on listed shares (with Securities Transaction Tax-STT paid) is taxed at 20 per cent under the Income Tax Act.

LTCG refer to the profits earned from the sale of capital assets that are held for a longer duration, beyond a specified minimum period defined by tax laws. The holding period depends on the type of asset:

- For listed equity shares, equity-oriented mutual funds and units of a business trust, the holding period must exceed 12 months.
- For real estate, gold and debt mutual funds, the asset must be held for more than 24 or 36 months, depending on the category.

LTCG is usually taxed at lower or concessional rates compared to short-term capital gains. For example, LTCG on listed shares exceeding ₹1 lakh is taxed at 12.5 per cent without indexation, as per current Indian tax laws. This tax benefit encourages long-term investments.

5. Income from Other Sources

A residual category covering earnings not included in the above heads, such as these:

- Interest (savings accounts, FD).
- Dividends, lottery winnings, gifts (beyond exempt limits).
- Rental income from plant, machinery, equipment etc.

Indexation is a method used in taxation to adjust the purchase price of an asset to account for inflation. This helps in calculating real gains rather than nominal gains when an asset is sold.

When you buy an asset (like property, gold or debt mutual funds), inflation may increase its value over time. Indexation allows you to adjust the original purchase price using a government-notified inflation index called the Cost Inflation Index (CII). This reduces your taxable capital gain.

Without Indexation (Applicable Rule):

- LTCG exceeding ₹1 lakh in a financial year is taxed at 12.5 per cent,
- No indexation benefit is allowed,
- This applies to listed equity shares, equity mutual funds and units of a business trust (as per Section 112A of the Income Tax Act).

Indexation is allowed for:

- Other assets such as real estate, gold, debt mutual funds (if applicable under old rules)
- These are taxed at 20% with indexation under Section 112.

Note: *Indexation does not apply to short-term capital gains (STCG). Since these gains are considered to be made in a short duration, inflation does not have a significant impact and therefore, no inflation adjustment (indexation) is allowed.*

KNOW THE DIFFERENCE: INCOME, SALARY, PROFIT AND MORE

Understanding the differences between terms like income, salary, profit, gross salary and cost to company (CTC) is essential for financial literacy. Some of these terms are often used interchangeably, but have distinct meanings in personal finance and taxation.

Taxable vs Non-Taxable Income

- **Taxable Income:** This is the portion liable to tax. This is earnings after adjustment of exemptions and deductions.
- **Non-taxable Income:** Agricultural income, Public Provident Fund/ Employees' Provident Fund (PPF/EPF) interest, tax-free bonds interest, gifts from relatives (within limits), scholarships.

Note: In EPF, both the employee and the employer contribute 12 per cent of basic salary or basic salary plus dearness allowance (DA) each month. Contributions qualify for tax deduction under section 80C and withdrawals are tax-free after five years of continuous service.

Income vs. Profit

- **Income:** Broad term covering all types of earnings (salary, business revenue, rent, investments, all).
- **Profit:** Specifically denotes surplus after deducting business expenses (gross/net profit).

Salary vs. Income

- **Salary:** Fixed compensation received from an employer; it is a part of total income.
- **Income:** All earnings, including salary, investments, rentals and business profits.

Gross Salary vs Net Salary

- **Gross Salary:** Total earnings before deductions (taxes, PF, insurance). It includes basic pay, allowances and bonuses.
- **Net Salary (Take-home):** Gross salary minus statutory and voluntary deductions. It reflects the actual disposable income available for personal use.
- Calculated as
  Net Salary = Gross Salary - (Income Tax + EPF + Professional Tax + Other Deductions)

Understanding this distinction helps employees plan their monthly budgets more effectively, assess job offers with greater clarity and make informed decisions to optimize their tax-planning strategies.

- Statutory Deductions: These are mandatory deductions from an employee's salary as required by law. Employers must deduct and deposit them with the relevant authorities. Examples: EPF, professional tax, income tax or tax deducted at source (TDS), employees' state insurance (ESI).
- Voluntary Deductions: These are optional deductions made with the employee's consent, often for personal or organizational benefits.
- Examples: Voluntary Provident Fund (VPF), loan repayments to the employer, contributions to charitable funds, group insurance premium.

Salary vs Cost to Company (CTC)

- **Salary:** Direct employee earnings (basic + allowances).
- **CTC:** Employer's total expenditure on an employee, including direct benefits (basic salary, allowances), indirect benefits (PF, gratuity, insurance) and variable pay (bonuses, incentives).

Key differences:

Aspect	Salary	CTC
Composition	Take-home pay + deductions	All company expenses on employee
Visibility	Appears in payslip	May not be fully visible
Tax Impact	Only taxable components considered	Includes non-taxable elements

For example, an employee with ₹8 lakh CTC might have

- ₹6 lakh gross salary
- ₹5 lakh net salary after deductions

Remaining ₹2 lakh in CTC goes to employer's contribution to PF, gratuity, insurance, etc.

UNDERSTANDING SALARY COMPONENTS: GROSS VS NET SALARY AND CTC

Components of Gross Salary

Gross salary is the total compensation an employee earns before any deduction. It includes multiple components that together form an employee's complete remuneration package:

1. Basic Salary

The core fixed amount paid to an employee, excluding bonuses, incentives or additional benefits. It typically forms 40-50 per cent of the total salary and serves as the basis for calculating other components.

2. House Rent Allowance (HRA)

A component designed to cover housing expenses. It is a part of the salary provided by employers to help employees meet the cost of renting a house. HRA is partially or fully exempt from tax under certain conditions.

3. Employees' Provident Fund (EPF)

A mandatory retirement benefit where both employer and employee contribute 12% of the basic salary each month.

4. Perquisites

Non-cash benefits provided by employers. These may be taxable or exempt based on government regulations and may include:

- Company-leased accommodation
- Personal driver
- Club memberships
- Stock options

5. Special Arrears

Additional payments are made when an employee receives a salary increment retrospectively. These are taxed in the year they are received rather than when they become due.

For instance, if an employee is granted a salary hike in March 2025, effective from April 2024, the difference in salary from April 2024 to February 2025 is paid as arrears. These arrears are taxable in the financial year in which they are received (i.e., 2024–2025), not when they became due. However, the employee can claim relief under section 89(1) to reduce the tax burden caused by the lump sum receipt.

6. Special Allowances

Various supplementary payments of which here are some examples:

- Transport Allowance
- Conveyance Allowance
- Leave Travel Allowance (LTA)
- Outstation Allowance

7. Bonus

Performance-based or fixed payments are given annually or periodically. Statutory bonuses are mandatory for certain industries under the Payment of Bonus Act, 1965.

8. Professional Tax

A state-level tax is deducted at source, typically ranging from ₹200 to ₹2,500 annually, depending on the state.

9. Income Tax

It is calculated based on the employee's income slab and investment declarations. Then TDS is deducted monthly from the salary.

COMPONENTS EXCLUDED FROM GROSS SALARY

Certain benefits are not part of gross salary calculations:

- Medical expense reimbursements (up to ₹15,000 annually tax-free)
- Leave travel concession
- Gratuity payments (tax-exempt up to ₹20 lakh)

- Employer-provided meals (free food up to ₹50 per meal exempt)
- Leave encashment (tax rules vary based on circumstances)

TRACKING TAX DEDUCTIONS

Employees should regularly verify their tax deductions through these:

1. Form 16

- Issued by the employer annually
- Contains details of
- ■ exemptions claimed.
- Must verify:
- ■ PAN and TAN details of the employee and the employer
- ■ TDS amounts match actual deposits

> ➢ Form 16 is typically divided into two parts:
> - Part A: Contains TDS details, PAN, TAN and employer–employee information
> - Part B: Contains salary breakup and tax computation
>
> ➢ Tax Deduction and Collection Account Number (TAN) is a 10-digit alphanumeric number issued by the Income Tax Department of India to individuals or entities responsible for deducting or collecting tax at source (TDS or TCS).

2. Form 26AS

- Consolidated tax statement available on the Income Tax portal
- What it shows:
- ■ All TDS deductions against PAN
- ■ Tax deposits by the employer
- ■ Advance tax payments

- Annual Information Report (AIR) transactions

What Regular Checks Ensure

- No overpayment of taxes
- Proper credit for all deductions
- Compliance with tax regulations

Practical Implications of Tracking Tax Deductions

1. **Job Offer Evaluation**
- Compare CTC breakdowns across offers
- Assess actual take-home pay differences
2. **Tax Planning**
- Structure allowances optimally (e.g., maximizing HRA exemption)
- Timely investments to reduce TDS deductions
3. **Financial Planning**
- Budget based on net salary
- Account for mandatory deductions in savings plans

Understanding these salary components empowers employees to make informed financial decisions and maximize their earnings potential while remaining tax-compliant.

CHAPTER 5

PERSONAL BUDGETING – MANAGING HOME AND EXPENDITURE

A budget is a structured financial plan that helps individuals allocate their income towards expenses, savings and investments. Just as governments prepare annual budgets by considering income and expenditure, individuals must manage their finances systematically to ensure financial stability and growth.

WHY BUDGETING MATTERS

- Helps to track income and expenses
- Ensures disciplined spending habits
- Prepares for emergencies and future goals
- Reduces financial stress by avoiding debt traps

THE 50/30/20 BUDGETING RULE

A simple yet effective method to manage finances, the 50/30/20 rule divides post-tax income into three categories:

1. 50 per cent for Needs (Essential Expenses)

These are generally non-negotiable expenses required for survival and basic living:

- Housing (rent, mortgage, property tax)
- Utilities (electricity, water, gas, internet)
- Groceries and essential household items
- Loan EMIs (home, car, education)
- Insurance premiums (health, term, motor)

- Basic healthcare and medicines
- School, tuition and hostel fees for children

If needs exceed 50 per cent:

- Consider cost-cutting (e.g., refinancing loans, reducing utility bills)
- Explore cheaper housing alternatives
- Increase income through some extra work or a side business

2. 30 per cent for Wants (Lifestyle Expenses)

These are discretionary expenses that enhance quality of life but are not essential:

- Entertainment (OTT subscriptions, movies, concerts)
- Dining out and food delivery
- Shopping (clothes, gadgets, luxury items)
- Travel and vacations
- Hobbies and fitness membership

Managing Wants:

- Choose budget-friendly alternatives (e.g., home workouts instead of paying for a gym memberships)
- Avoid impulsive purchases by using a 'cooling-off period'
- Limit credit card usage for entertainment-related spending

3. 20 per cent for Savings and Investments

This portion secures financial stability and future goals:

- Emergency fund (3-6 months of living expenses)
- Investments (mutual funds, stocks, PPF, NPS, gold)
- Retirement planning (EPF, pension schemes)
- Debt prepayment (reducing high-interest loans)

Maximizing Savings:

- Automate investments via Systematic Investment Plans (SIPs)
- Prioritize high-yield, tax-efficient instruments (ELSS, NPS)
- Review and adjust investment time to time

- **Equity-Linked Savings Scheme (ELSS)** is a type of mutual fund that invests mainly in stocks and offers tax benefits under Section 80C.
- Lock-in period: Three years (shortest among tax-saving options)
- Returns: Market-linked, potentially higher
- Ideal for: Those looking for long-term wealth creation with tax savings
- **National Pension System (NPS)** is a government-backed retirement savings scheme that helps you build a pension corpus.
- Tax benefit: Available under section 80CCD (1) and additional ₹50,000 under 80CCD (1B)
- Returns: Market-linked but relatively stable
- Lock-in: Till retirement age (60 years)
- Ideal for: Salaried and self-employed individuals focused on long-term retirement planning

STEPS TO IMPLEMENT THE 50/30/20 RULE

1. Calculate Post-Tax Income

- Salaried individuals: Take-home salary after TDS, PF and other deductions.
- Self-employed: Net income after business expenses and tax provisions.

2. Track and Categorize Expenses

- Use budgeting apps (Walnut, ET Money) or spreadsheets.
- Review bank statements to identify spending patterns.

3. Allocate Funds Based on 50/30/20

- Adjust percentages if necessary (e.g., 60/20/20 for high-cost cities).
- Prioritize needs first, then savings, before allocating to wants.

4. Evaluate and Optimize Monthly

- Identify overspending areas (e.g., dining out, subscriptions).
- Shift excess funds from 'wants' to 'savings' for better financial growth.

ALTERNATIVE BUDGETING STRATEGIES

Do not assume that the 50/30/20 rule is the only option. If it does not suit your financial situation, consider other combinations based on your needs and goals. Here are some more options:

1. 70/20/10 Rule

- 70 per cent for living expenses
- 20 per cent for savings and debt repayment
- 10 per cent for investments

2. Zero-Based Budgeting

- Assign every rupee a purpose (income – expenses = zero).
- Ideal for meticulous spenders

3. Envelope System

- Allocating cash into envelopes for different spending categories
- Helps curb overspending

MANAGING FINANCES DURING UNCERTAIN TIMES

1. Build a Strong Emergency Fund

- Save at least six months' worth of essential expenses
- Keep funds in liquid assets (savings account, liquid mutual funds)

2. Reduce Non-Essential Spending

- Pause discretionary expenses (travel, luxury purchases)
- Renegotiate bills (broadband, insurance premiums)

3. Focus on Debt Management

- Prioritize high-interest debt repayment (credit cards, personal loans)
- Opt for loan moratoriums or restructuring if needed

4. Diversify Income Sources

- Freelancing, part-time gigs or passive income (rentals, dividends).

ASSET ALLOCATION AND PORTFOLIO REBALANCING

Asset allocation is the process of dividing your investments across different asset classes (like equity, debt and gold) to balance risk and reward. Whereas portfolio rebalancing means adjusting your investments periodically to maintain your target allocations as market values change.

1. Ideal Asset Allocation

Risk Profile	Equity	Debt	Gold/Other
Conservative	30%	60%	10%
Moderate	50%	40%	10%
Aggressive	70%	20%	10%

2. Rebalancing Strategies

- Annual Review: Adjust allocations based on market performance.
- Tax Efficiency: Harvest tax losses to offset gains.
- Goal-Based Adjustments: Shift from equity to debt as you approach your financial goals.

Taxation and Budgeting

- Use tax-saving instruments (80C, 80D, HRA, LTA).
- File ITR on time to avoid penalties.
- Optimize capital gains tax by holding investments for the long term.

FINANCIAL RESILIENCE: MANAGING MONEY DURING UNCERTAIN TIMES

Financial resilience means being prepared to handle unexpected situations like job loss, medical emergencies or economic downturns. While building an emergency fund, reducing non-essential expenses and avoiding new debt are key steps to maintain financial stability during such times.

1. Building a Contingency Fund

A contingency fund acts as a financial safety net for unexpected events such as medical emergencies, job loss or urgent repairs.

Key Considerations:

- Size of Fund: Save three to six months' worth of living expenses (longer if you have dependents).
- Liquidity: Keep funds in liquid assets (savings account, liquid mutual funds, short-term FDs).
- Start Small: Begin with a small amount and gradually increase contributions.

> Warren Buffett once wisely said, 'Do not save what is left after spending; spend what is left after saving.'

2. Smart Investing for Long-Term Growth

Investing early harnesses the power of compounding, where returns generate more returns over time.

Best Practices:

- SIPs: Invest fixed amounts monthly in mutual funds for disciplined wealth creation.
- Diversify: Spread investments across equity, debt, gold and real estate to reduce risk.
- Avoid Emotional Investing: Stick to a plan instead of reacting to market fluctuations.

3. Debt Management Strategies

High debt can cripple financial stability. Follow these steps to stay in control:

a) Limit Debt Burden

- Spend no more than 10 per cent of your income on EMIs/credit card bills.
- Prioritize high-interest debt repayment (credit cards > personal loans > home loans).

b) Improve Credit Score

- Pay EMIs on time to avoid penalties.
- Maintain a credit utilization ratio below 30 per cent.
- A good credit score (750+) ensures lower loan interest rates.

c) Prepay Loans Early

- Saves thousands in interest over time.
- Reinvest savings for better returns.

4. Asset Allocation and Portfolio Rebalancing

A well-structured portfolio balances risk and returns based on financial goals.

Optimal Allocation Guide:

Rebalancing Tips:

- Review every 6-12 months.
- Book profits in overperforming assets (e.g., stocks) and reinvest in underperforming ones.
- Adjust based on changing goals or risk appetite.

5. Tax-Efficient Financial Planning

Smart tax planning reduces liabilities while growing wealth.

Key Tax-Saving Instruments:

Key Tax-Saving Instruments:

- Section 80C (₹1.5 lakh deduction): ELSS, PPF, NSC, life insurance premiums.
- Section 80D (Health Insurance): Up to ₹1 lakh for family + parents.
- NPS (Additional ₹50,000 deduction under 80CCD(1B)).

Special Benefits:

- Senior Citizens (sixty-plus): They are eligible for higher interest rates on fixed deposits and enjoy higher tax-free interest limits.
- Women Investors: Certain schemes offer lower loan interest rates or higher returns for women and girl child accounts.

6. Avoiding Common Financial Mistakes

- Fear of Missing Out (FOMO): Do not chase trends; invest based on research.
- Impulsive Spending: Use budgeting apps to track expenses.
- Ignoring Insurance: Secure health and term insurance early for better premiums.

Now let's take a closer look at the idea of expenditure and purchase.

EXPENDITURE VS. PURCHASE

- Expenditure: Money spent on goods/services, recorded at the time of purchase (cash or credit)
- Purchase: Acquiring goods/services via payment (cash, credit); crucial in manufacturing (raw materials) and personal shopping

Basics	Expenditure	Purchase
Meaning	Money spent on goods or services	Act of acquiring goods or services through payment
Scope	Broader term, includes all kinds of spending (e.g., salaries, rent, purchases)	Narrower term, refers only to acquiring goods or services
Purpose	Can be for any business or personal expense	Primarily focused on obtaining goods or services
Timing	Recorded when money is spent or liability is incurred (cash or credit)	Recorded when the item is acquired, even if payment is delayed

Basics	Expenditure	Purchase
Relevance	Used in both financial accounting and budgeting	Especially important in inventory and manufacturing (e.g., raw material)
Examples	Paying salaries, rent, electricity bills and making purchases	Buying raw materials, office equipment, groceries or electronics

Goal Horizon	Equity (%)	Debt (%)	Gold/Other (%)
Short-Term (<3 yrs)	20–30	60–70	10
Medium-Term (3–7 yrs)	50–60	30–40	10
Long-Term (>7 yrs)	70–80	10–20	10

TRADITIONAL SHOPPING AND ONLINE SHOPPING

Traditionally, we are used to shopping by physically visiting stores to purchase items. This allows us to check the product in person, but such shopping is limited by store hours and location. However, with the increasing use of computers and the internet, shopping habits have changed significantly in recent years. Gradually we have become more accustomed to online shopping. By visiting specific websites or e-commerce platforms like Amazon or eBay, we can buy products using a card or opt for cash on delivery. Although we cannot physically inspect the product, online shopping offers the convenience of 24/7 access.

Traditional vs Online Shopping

Aspect	Traditional Shopping	Online Shopping
Advantages	Physical inspection of products	24/7 shopping, global access
	Immediate ownership	Price comparisons, discounts
	Easy returns, social experience	Home delivery, no travel costs
Disadvantages	Limited product range	No physical inspection before purchase
	Higher prices (store overheads)	Delivery delays, shipping fees
	Crowds, fixed store hours	Risk of fraud, security threats

Note: *High-value items (gold, cars, property) should always be inspected physically before purchase.*

HIRE PURCHASE VS INSTALMENT SYSTEM

Feature	Hire Purchase	Instalment Purchase
Ownership	Transfers only after final payment	Transfers immediately at purchase
Risk	Seller bears risk until full payment	Buyer assumes risk immediately
Default	Seller can repossess goods	Buyer retains ownership; legal action for dues

In a hire purchase agreement, the purchaser gains ownership of the goods only after paying all instalments. Until the final payment, the seller retains ownership and if the buyer defaults, the seller can repossess the goods without compensation.

In contrast, an instalment purchase system is a type of credit sale where the buyer receives both ownership and possession immediately but pays in instalments. If the buyer defaults, the seller cannot reclaim the goods but can only sue for the outstanding amount.

Before purchasing, verify whether the seller has repossession rights in case of default. This determines if the agreement is a hire purchase or an instalment purchase.

Your idea of purchase will never be complete without a clear understanding of these two terms below.

CHALLAN AND VOUCHER

A **Challan** is a document used to make or record payments, especially to banks or government authorities. It acts as proof that a payment has been made for a specific purpose, such as taxes, fees or penalties.

A **Voucher**, on the other hand, is a written document that serves as evidence of a business transaction. It records payments made or received and is commonly used in accounting. Vouchers can include cash vouchers, payment vouchers and purchase vouchers.

Types of Challan

Bank Challan: Used for depositing money (similar to a deposit slip but with pre-filled details).

Tax Challan: Official forms like ITNS 280/281 for tax payments.

Delivery Challan: Acts as proof of goods delivery, often signed by the receiver before payment.

1. **Income Tax Challan Form 280 (ITNS 280)** – Used by individuals and non-corporate taxpayers to pay income tax, advance tax, self-assessment tax and surcharge.
2. **Income Tax Challan Form 281 (ITNS 281)** – Used by deductors to deduct TDS and Tax Collected at Source (TCS) on behalf of the government.

Types of Voucher

Retail Vouchers: Prepaid codes (e.g., mobile recharge, e-vouchers for online shopping)

Accounting Vouchers: Documents supporting payments to vendors, including invoices, receipts or wage sheets

BUYING GOLD

Gold holds cultural significance in India, especially during weddings and festivals. However, buyers should exercise caution when purchasing gold jewellery.

1. **Check Gold Rates** – Prices vary by city due to taxes, transportation and local demand.
2. **Purity** – Measured in karats:

- 24K (100 per cent pure): Soft, used for coins/bars
- 22K (91.6 per cent pure): Common for jewellery
- 18K (75 per cent pure): Less expensive, mixed with alloys

4. **Hallmarking** – Mandatory in India; ensures purity (BIS-certified)

The **Bureau of Indian Standards (BIS)** ensures product quality and safety through different certification schemes:

- **BIS Hallmark** for gold and silver jewellery purity (22K, 18K).
- **ISI mark** for household and industrial items like LED lights, helmets and pressure cookers.
- **Compulsory Registration Scheme (CRS)** number for electronics items like mobile phones, power banks and smart TVs.
- **QR Code Verification** is new-age packaging that includes **QR** codes for easy online verification.

1. **Making Charges** – Making charges vary based on the design complexity and the jeweller. Typically, they range from 8 to 20 per cent of the gold ornament's value. When creating a new ornament

using old gold, the buyer often incurs some loss, as making charges are applied again.

2. **Wastage Charges** – Higher for intricate or stone-studded designs. Due to melting, cutting and shaping for designing the new ornament from old gold, there is some wastage of gold.
3. **Final Calculation** – Includes gold rate, making/wastage charges and gemstone value (if applicable).
4. **Festive Discounts** – Compare offers, but avoid impulsive buys if prices are inflated.
5. **Resale/Exchange** – Even in confirmed buyback policies, jewellers deduct making charges.
6. **Gold Schemes** – Instalment plans to ease purchases.
7. **Transparency** – Ensure proper billing (PAN for high-value purchases) for legal security.

PURCHASING A CAR

Buying a car is now achievable for India's middle class, but careful planning is essential.

1. **Budgeting** – Allocate ≤ 25 per cent of monthly income for car-related expenses. For budget purposes, the car value should include insurance, registration and maintenance.
2. **New vs. Used** – Assess ownership costs and suitability.
3. **Car Type** – Prioritize energy source (petrol/diesel /electric/hybrid), features and safety.
4. **Resale Value** – Opt for brands with good service networks and spare parts availability.
5. **Research** – Compare manufacturer's suggested retail price (MSRP) and dealer quotes.
6. **Financing** – Secure loans beforehand for better interest rates.
7. **Dealer Comparison** – Negotiate by exploring multiple dealers.
8. **Test Drive** – Evaluate comfort, handling and noise levels.

9. **Negotiation** – Focus on total cost, not monthly payments; avoid revealing trade-ins early.
10. **Insurance** – Factor premiums into the total cost (high for luxury/theft-prone models).
11. **Avoid Add-ons** – Avoid unnecessary dealer add-ons, e.g., extended warranties or optional accessories.
12. **Pre-owned Car Checks** – check the condition of the car with the help of an expert mechanic; verify Registration Certificate, Pollution Under Control certificate and insurance papers.
13. **Legal Checks** – Ensure no pending accidents, police cases or unpaid EMIs.
14. **Ownership Transfer** – Complete the Regional Transport Office (RTO) Form 29/30 for a smooth transfer.

Avoid impulsive decisions; research thoroughly to make a financially sound purchase.

PURCHASING LAND OR HOUSE PROPERTY

Buying a house or land is a lifelong dream and a major financial decision. Even if funds are insufficient, home loans can help, as paying EMIs is better than paying rent. However, thorough research and careful consideration are essential before investing in real estate.

Key Factors to Consider Before Buying Property

1. **Budget** – Determine how much you can afford, considering savings, income and loan eligibility. So calculate the amount you can put down as a down payment and can afford to give EMI for the next few years. Ensure EMIs do not exceed 30–40 per cent of your monthly income.
2. **Hidden Costs** – Beyond the property price, account for:

- Brokerage fees
- Home loan processing charges
- Stamp duty and registration fees

- Interior decoration costs
- Annual maintenance charges

3. **Location** – Prime locations appreciate faster and ensure better rental demand. Check proximity to schools, hospitals, offices and markets. Evaluate safety, infrastructure and connectivity.
4. **Water and Power Supply** – Ensure the area has reliable water and power supplies, and sewage infrastructure. Talk to residents to verify claims made by builders.
5. **Safety and Security** – Opt for gated communities with 24/7 security, CCTV surveillance and emergency measures like fire safety systems.
6. **Amenities** – Check for elevators, parks, gyms and parking facilities. Even if not within the complex, nearby amenities add value.
7. **Legal Verification** – Ensure the property has:

- Real Estate Regulatory Authority (RERA) registration (for under-construction properties)
- Clear title deed and sales deed
- No-Objection Certificates (NOC) from authorities
- Proper land records and soil quality reports

8. **Builder's Reputation** – Research the developer's track record for timely delivery, quality construction and legal compliance. Consult a lawyer before signing agreements.
9. **Home Loan Options** – Compare interest rates, processing fees and prepayment penalties before finalizing a loan.
10. **TDS for Non-resident Indian (NRI) Sellers** – If buying from an NRI, deduct TDS as per tax laws.
11. **Home Insurance** – Protect your investment with insurance covering structural damage and contents.

Mutation, Registration and Stamp Duty

- **Mutation (Dakhil Kharij)** – Updates ownership records in government revenue files. Required after purchase, inheritance or transfer.

- **Registration** – Legally transfers ownership at the sub-registrar's office after paying stamp duty.
- **Stamp Duty** – A state government tax based on property value, location and age. Non-payment leads to penalties.

Mutation, Registration Difference:

- **Registration** proves ownership.
- **Mutation** updates tax records and follows the registration, but it does not confer ownership.

Maintenance Charges for Apartments

- Calculated per square feet, depending on amenities (lifts, security, gyms, etc.).
- Higher charges usually mean better facilities.
- As there is generally no strict legal binding regarding maintenance charges, conflicts are common among co-owners in an apartment. Every flat owner should remember that living in a shared community requires cooperation, which ultimately benefits everyone in the long run. If disputes arise over maintenance charges, it is important to resolve them amicably and transparently. This may involve open communication, reviewing the society's bylaws or seeking mediation.

EDAAKHIL PORTAL

Launched by the National Consumer Disputes Redressal Commission (NCDRC), eDaakhil allows online consumer complaint filings under the Consumer Protection Act, 2019. This portal simplifies grievance redressal, eliminating the need for physical visits to consumer courts.

Features:

- Paperless complaints with online fee payment.
- Track case status digitally.
- Available across India, from metro cities to remote rural areas

How to Use:

1. Register via OTP on the mobile phone /email of the consumer
2. File complaints, pay fees and monitor progress online.

REAL ESTATE REGULATORY AUTHORITY (RERA)

India's real estate sector, while vast and lucrative, has long been plagued by fraudulent practices, project delays and abandoned constructions. To protect homebuyers and bring transparency to the industry, the Indian government enacted the Real Estate (Regulation and Development) Act (RERA) in 2016. Real Estate Regulatory Authority is established in different states by this Act to regulate this sector.

Key Objectives of RERA

1. **Regulation & Accountability** – Ensures builders adhere to approved plans and timelines.
2. **Transparency** – It mandates the disclosure of project details, approvals and financials.
3. **Buyer Protection** – Safeguards buyers from fraud, delays and unfair practices.
4. **Dispute Resolution** – Provides a fast and structured grievance redressal system.

How RERA Works

- **Mandatory Registration** – All residential and commercial projects (on land exceeding 500 sq. meters or eight units) must register with RERA before sale.
- **State-Level Authorities** – Each state has its own RERA body; buyers should verify project registration on the respective state's RERA website.
- **Financial Safeguards** – Developers must deposit 70 per cent of buyer funds in a dedicated account, ensuring money is used only for construction.

Key Provisions Under RERA

1. **Advance Payment Limit**

- Builders cannot demand more than 10 per cent of the property cost before signing a sale agreement.

2. Carpet Area Definition

- Properties must be sold based on carpet area (actual usable space), not super built-up area (which includes common spaces).

3. Project Delays & Compensation

- If a project is delayed, buyers can:
  - Claim a full refund with interest.
  - Demand compensation for losses

4. Structural Defects Liability

- Builders must repair any structural defects if it is within five years of purchase and rectify them within thirty days of complaint.

5. No Unapproved Changes

- Developers cannot alter project plans (layout, design, specifications) without buyer consent.

6. Mandatory Registration for Advertisements

- Every real estate advertisement must mention the RERA registration number; unregistered projects are illegal.

GRIEVANCE REDRESSAL MECHANISM

Step 1: File a complaint with the state RERA authority.

Step 2: If unsatisfied, appeal to the RERA Appellate Tribunal.

Step 3: Further appeals can be made in high courts.

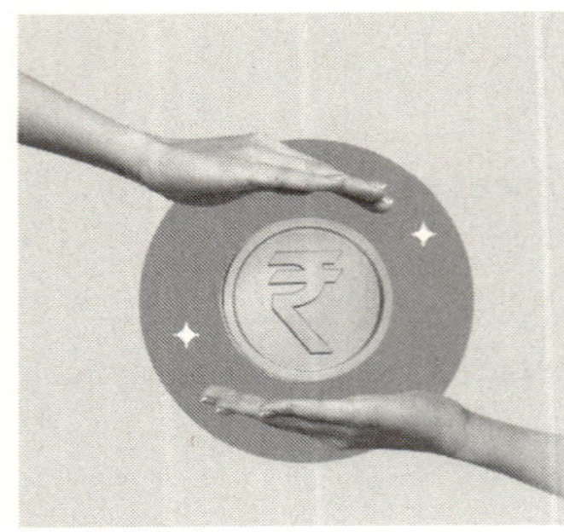

CHAPTER 6

IDEA OF TAXES AND DUTIES

Taxes and **duties** are compulsory financial contributions levied by governments to support public services and manage economic activity. Although the terms are often used interchangeably, they serve different purposes within a country's fiscal policy.

Key Differences between Tax and Duty

Aspect	Tax	Duty
Definition	Compulsory charge on income/profits or consumption	Levy on goods (manufactured/ imported)
Purpose	Funds public expenditure (e.g., infrastructure)	Regulates trade, protects domestic industries
Payment Type	Direct (e.g., Income Tax) or Indirect (e.g., Goods and Services Tax -GST)	Always indirect (e.g., Customs Duty)
Applicability	Individuals/ businesses (based on income)	Specific goods/ services (production/ import)

Aspect	Tax	Duty
Impact	Affects income inequality, spending behaviour	Influences market prices, trade competition
Revision	Adjusted in annual budgets	Modified per trade policies / international agreements

TYPES OF TAXES

Direct Taxes

- Paid directly to the government by individuals/businesses
- Example: Income Tax (administered by CBDT)

Indirect Taxes

- Collected via intermediaries (e.g., sellers)
- Example: GST (governed by CBIC)

Penalties: Tax evasion is punishable by law. Late payment attracts a penalty

➢ The Central Board of Direct Taxes (CBDT) is the top policy-making body for direct taxes in India, such as income tax and corporate tax. It functions under the Ministry of Finance and is responsible for tax policy formulation, administration and enforcement. The CBDT also supervises the Income Tax Department and ensures the effective implementation of tax laws across the country.

➢ The Central Board of Indirect Taxes and Customs (CBIC) is the apex body for administering indirect taxes in India. It operates under the Ministry of Finance, Government of India.

Key Functions of CBIC:

- Formulation and implementation of policies related to Goods and Services Tax (GST), Customs and Central Excise.

- Administration of laws related to imports, exports and anti-smuggling.
- Oversight of GST compliance, refunds, audits and taxpayer services.
- Management of India's customs border controls and facilitation of international trade.

TYPES OF DUTIES

- **Customs Duty:** Levied on imported/exported goods
- **Excise Duty:** Charged on domestically manufactured goods

Objective: Protect local industries and control trade flows.

4. ASSESSMENT YEAR (AY) VS. FINANCIAL YEAR (FY)

- **Financial Year (FY):** Period of earning income (1 April–31 March).
- **Assessment Year (AY):** Year in which FY income is taxed.
- **Example:** Income earned in **FY 2024–25** is taxed in **AY 2025–26.**

KEY CHANGE (2025 BUDGET):

- **Tax Year** replaces FY/AY for simplicity.
- Aligns income earnings and assessment under one 12-month period (April–March).
- Exceptions: For new businesses / any new source (rent or investment), start from the activation date.
- **FY retains relevance** for legal deadlines/audits.

RESIDENTIAL STATUS IN INDIA: KEY CONSIDERATIONS FOR TAX LIABILITY

Your residential status in India is crucial as it defines what portion of your income is taxable or not under the Income Tax Act, 1961. Your status depends on the duration of your stay in India during a financial year (1 April–31 March) and the preceding years. Different categories of residential status are discussed below:

Resident of India

An individual qualifies as a Resident if they meet either of the following conditions:

1. Stay in India for 182 days or more during the financial year.
2. Stay for 60 days or more in that financial year and 365 days or more in last four years.

Exceptions:

- **Indian Citizens taking up Employment Abroad:** The 60-day rule extends to 182 days in the year of departure.
- **Indian Citizens/Persons of Indian Origin (PIOs) Visiting India:**
  - Normally, they must stay 182 days or more to be considered a resident.
  - If their Indian income (excluding foreign earnings) exceeds ₹15 lakh, the threshold reduces to 120 days.

Summary:

- 182 days or more in India → Resident.
- 60 days or more (current year) + 365 days or more (last 4 years) → Resident.
- For NRIs visiting India, 182+ days (or 120– days if Indian income > ₹15 lakh) rule applies.

ROR VS RNOR

Once classified as a resident, further categorization depends on prior years' stay:

Resident and Ordinarily Resident (ROR):

- Must meet both conditions:

1. Resident in 2 out of the last 10 years.
2. Stayed in India for 730 days or more in the previous 7 years.

Resident but Not Ordinarily Resident (RNOR):

Applies if any of these conditions are met:

1. Non-resident for 9 out of the last 10 years.
2. Stayed less than or equal to 729 days in the last 7 years.

3. Indian citizen/PIO with Indian income greater than ₹15 lakh, staying 120-182 days.
4. Deemed resident under Section 6 (1A).

DEEMED RESIDENT

Introduced in 2020, this applies to Indian citizens who

1. Earn greater than ₹15 lakh from Indian sources (excluding foreign income),
2. They are not taxable in any other country due to residency rules.

Implications:

- Treated as RNOR (only Indian income is taxed).
- Global income remains non-taxable unless derived from India.
- Must file an ITR if taxable income exceeds exemption limits.

Example: An Indian working in a tax-free country (e.g., UAE) with ₹20 lakh Indian rental income qualifies as a Deemed Resident. Only the ₹20 lakh is taxed in India.

NON-RESIDENT (NRI)

Fails to meet any residency conditions. Taxed only on income from India.

RESIDENTIAL STATUS FOR ENTITIES

- **Companies:** Resident if incorporated in India or effectively managed from India.
- **Firms/LLPs/AOPs:** Resident if control and management are in India.

TAX IMPLICATIONS

- **Resident (ROR):** Global income taxable.
- **RNOR/Deemed Resident:** Only Indian income + certain foreign income.
- **Non-Resident:** Only India-sourced income.

- A **Limited Liability Partnership (LLP)** is a hybrid legal structure that combines elements of both a company and a traditional partnership.
  Key Features:
  - Separate a legal entity from its partners
  - Limited liability for each partner (personal assets are protected)
  - Flexibility in internal structure and management
  - Commonly used by professionals like lawyers, accountants, consultants, and startups.
- An **Association of Persons (AOP)** is a group of individuals or entities that come together to earn income, typically for a specific purpose or business activity.
  Key Features:
  - Not necessarily a separate legal entity
  - Can include individuals, firms, companies, etc.
  - Taxed as a single unit under the Income Tax Act
  - Formed voluntarily, often for a temporary or joint venture project

UNDERSTANDING TAN, PAN, GST AND TDS IN INDIA

Tax Deduction and Collection Account Number (TAN)

The TAN is a 10-digit alphanumeric identifier. The Income Tax Department issues it to individuals or entities responsible for TDS or TCS.

Key Features:

- Mandatory for TDS/TCS filings under Section 203A of the Income Tax Act, 1961.
- Penalties apply for non-compliance:
- Section 272BB (1): Failure to obtain TAN – penalty up to ₹10,000.

- Section 272BB (2): Quoting incorrect TAN – penalty up to ₹10,000.

Application Process:

- Can be applied online or offline.
- Two types of applications:

1. New TAN allotment.
2. Correction/update in existing TAN.

Permanent Account Number (PAN)

The PAN is a unique 10-digit alphanumeric identifier. It is issued by the Income Tax department for taxpayers for tracking financial transactions.

Key Features:

- Acts as a universal tax ID for all financial activities (tax payments, investments, etc.).
- **Mandatory for:**
- Filing income tax returns.
- High-value transactions (property, investments, bank deposits).
- Business registrations.
- PAN card includes holder's name, photo, date of birth and PAN.
- Linking PAN with Aadhaar is compulsory.

Consequences of Multiple PANs:

- Illegal under Section 139A – penalty of ₹10,000 (Section 272B).
- Financial complications such as loan rejections, tax scrutiny, and credit score issues.
- Solution: Surrender duplicate PANs via the NSDL/UTIITSL portal.

Uses of PAN:

- Income tax filing
- Opening Bank Accounts
- Property transactions
- Business registrations
- Claiming tax refunds

National Securities Depository Limited (NSDL) and UTI Infrastructure Technology and Services Limited (UTIITSL) are authorized agencies for PAN-related services under the Income Tax Department.

Key Services Offered:

- Apply for a new PAN card
- Update or correct PAN details
- Track PAN card status
- Download e-PAN
- Link PAN with Aadhaar

Where to Access?

- **NSDL Portal:** https://www.tin-nsdl.com
- **UTIITSL Portal:** https://www.pan.utiitsl.com

Who Can Use These?

- Individuals
- Companies
- LLPs/AOPs
- NRIs

Benefit

These portals provide a secure, government-recognized online platform for PAN-related services, ensuring convenience and transparency.

Goods and Services Tax (GST)

GST is an indirect tax replacing multiple taxes (VAT, excise, service tax) since 1 July 2017.

Structure:

- Central Goods and Services Tax (CGST): The tax collected by the Central government on intra-state (within the same state)
- State Goods and Services Tax/Union Territory Goods and Services Tax (SGST/UTGST): SGST is levied by the state government on intra-state supply, while UTGST is levied by the Union Territory Government in Union Territories without a legislature (like Chandigarh or Lakshadweep) on intra-UT supplies.
- Integrated Goods and Services Tax (IGST): It is levied by the Central government on inter-state supply of goods and services (between two states or a state and a union territory). IGST also applies to imports and exports. The revenue collected under IGST

is shared between the Centre and the destination state where the goods or services are consumed.

- GST Identification Number (GSTIN): It is a 15-digit unique identification number assigned to every business or individual registered under the GST system in India.

Structure of GSTIN:

- **First 2 digits:** Represent the **state code.**
- **Next 10 digits**: Correspond to the **PAN** of the business.
- **13th digit**: Indicates the **number of registrations** under the same PAN in a state.
- **14th digit:** Defaulted as **'Z'**.
- **15th digit:** A **check code** used for validation.

Verify GSTIN via www.gst.gov.in.

GST Council:

- Headed by the finance minister of India (with the finance ministers of all states).
- Decides tax rates, exemptions and compliance rules.

Exclusions from GST:

- Petroleum products (petrol, diesel, natural gas).
- Alcohol for human consumption (other taxes apply).

Tax Deducted at Source (TDS)

TDS is a tax collection mechanism where a deductor (payer) withholds tax before making payments to a deductee (recipient). Then the deductor must deposit the deducted amount in the account of the tax authority. Whereas at the time of the returning tax file, the deductee will get a refund or that amount will be adjusted with their tax liability.

Applicability:

Salaries, interest, rent, professional fees, commissions.

Deducted as per prescribed rates. TDS rate varies

Consequences of Non-compliance:

- **Late Filing (Section 234E):** ₹200/day penalty (max: TDS amount).
- **Non-deposit (Section 276B):** 3 months – 7 years imprisonment + fine.

- **30 per cent Disallowance:** If TDS is not deducted, 30 per cent expense is added back to the income.
- **Interest @ 1.5 per cent per month** for delayed deposits.

Exceptions:

- **Rent payments** (unless exceeding ₹50,000/month).
- **Professional fees** (lawyer/doctor fees not exceeding ₹30,000/ transaction).

  In certain situations, for example, if an individual income taxpayer claims HRA exemption but fails to deduct TDS on rent paid, they may receive an income tax notice. This typically depends on the amount of rent paid and the residential status of the landlord. In such cases, it is advisable to consult a tax consultant, as applicable rates and conditions are subject to change from time to time.

Best Practices:

- File TDS returns within the due date to avoid penalties.
- Regularly verify Form 26AS to ensure accurate reflection of TDS credits.
- If excess TDS has been deducted, claim a refund while filing your Income Tax Return (ITR).

INCOME TAX RETURN (ITR) IN INDIA: A COMPREHENSIVE GUIDE

Filing an ITR is a legal obligation for individuals and entities whose income exceeds the specified threshold. It helps the government assess your tax liability and ensures transparency in your financial records. ITR filing also enables you to claim deductions, get refunds, and act as valid proof of income for loans or visa applications.

What is an ITR?

An ITR is a formal declaration filed by taxpayers with the Income Tax Department of India, disclosing their income, deductions, exemptions and taxes paid for a financial year (1 April to 31 March). Filing an ITR helps to determine your tax liability and enables tax refunds if excess tax has been paid.

It is mandatory for:

- Individuals
- Hindu Undivided Families (HUFs)
- Firms & LLPs
- Companies
- Other entities earning taxable income

Types of ITR Forms

The CBDT has prescribed different ITR forms based on income sources and taxpayer categories:

ITR Form	Applicable To
ITR-1 (Sahaj)	Salaried individuals with income up to ₹50 lakh (from salary, one house property, other sources).
ITR-2	Individuals/HUFs with income from capital gains, multiple house properties, foreign assets.
ITR-3	Professionals/business owners (sole proprietors, freelancers).
ITR-4 (Sugam)	Small businesses/individuals under presumptive taxation (income up to ₹50 lakh).
ITR-5	Firms, LLPs, AOPs, BOIs.
ITR-6	Companies not claiming tax exemption.
ITR-7	Trusts, political parties and charitable institutions.

Note: Choosing the correct form is crucial to avoid rejection.

Documents Required for ITR Filing

- PAN Card & Aadhaar (linked with PAN).
- Form 16 (for salaried employees – TDS details from employer).

- Form 16A/16B/16C (TDS on non-salary income like FD interest, rent, property sale).
- Form 26AS (Consolidated tax statement showing TDS, advance tax and refunds).
- Bank statements and investment proofs (for deductions under Section 80C– 80U).
- Capital gains statements (if applicable).

How to File ITR?

1. Online (E-filing):

Visit **incometax.gov.in**.

Select the correct ITR form based on income sources.

Fill in details, upload documents and submit.

E-verification using Aadhaar OTP, net banking or sending a signed copy to CPC Bengaluru.

2. Offline (Physical Submission):
   - Download the ITR form (JSON/Excel format).
   - Fill and submit to the Income Tax Office.

Consequences of Not Filing ITR

Failing to file ITR can lead to:

1. Penalties:
   - **Late filing fee (Section 234F):** currently ₹1,000 (if filed by 31 December) / ₹5,000 (after 31 December).
   - **Interest (Section 234A):** 1 per cent per month on unpaid tax.
   - No tax refunds if excess TDS was deducted.
   - Cannot carry forward losses (business/capital gains) to future years.
3. Financial & Legal Issues:
- Loan/visa rejections (banks/embassies require ITR as income proof).
- Legal action for tax evasion (prosecution under the Income Tax Act).

Impact of Taxes on Prices

Taxes and duties directly affect product/service prices:

Goods & Services Tax (GST):

- Prices may be 'exclusive of GST' (e.g., restaurant menus).
- **CGST + SGST** (intra-state) or **IGST** (inter-state) applies.

Customs & Excise Duties:

- Import duty changes (e.g., electronics, fuel) impact retail prices.
- Petrol/Diesel prices vary by state due to different VAT rates.

Budget Announcements:

- Tax hikes increase prices (e.g., cigarettes, luxury cars).
- Tax cuts reduce prices (e.g., mobile phones, essential goods).

SAVING, INVESTMENT AND WEALTH CREATION

CHAPTER 7

DIFFERENT SAVING AND INVESTMENT OPTIONS

Saving and investing form the foundation of sound personal finance. Saving helps build financial security for immediate and short-term needs, while investing focuses on long-term wealth creation and financial independence. Both are essential activities for achieving lasting financial well-being. Although people often use the terms interchangeably, saving and investing serve different purposes and complement each other in building a stable financial future. Such as for:

- Financial Security: Savings provide a safety net during emergencies.
- Wealth Creation: Investments grow money through compounding and higher returns.
- Goal Achievement: Saving supports short-term needs, investing funds for long-term goals.
- Inflation Protection: Investments help preserve purchasing power.
- Financial Independence: Consistent saving and investing reduce reliance on loans.

Difference between saving and investing

Saving refers to setting aside a portion of income for future use instead of spending it immediately. It acts as a financial safety net, ensuring funds are available for emergencies or future expenses. For example, keeping money in a bank account is a form of saving.

Investment, on the other hand, involves allocating money into assets such as stocks, bonds or real estate with the expectation of generating returns over time. Unlike saving, investment aims to grow wealth by taking calculated risks.

Short-term vs long-term financial goals

Short-term financial goals are those that you plan to achieve in the near future, generally within one to three years. Examples include building an emergency fund, paying off credit card debt, saving for a family trip or creating a contingency reserve. Because the time horizon is short, these goals often involve low-risk investments or savings instruments like FDs, RDs or liquid mutual funds, where funds remain easily accessible.

Long-term financial goals span a much longer time frame, typically more than five years and often extend to decades. They involve significant financial commitments and are closely tied to life milestones. Common examples include buying a home, children's higher education or retirement planning. These goals require sustained investment strategies, where compounding plays a key role. Long-term goals may involve equity investments, provident fund contributions or other growth-oriented instruments that can withstand short-term market fluctuations but provide higher returns over time.

Post Office Schemes

- Government-backed saving and investment options that provide safety and stable returns.
- Suitable for both short-term and long-term financial goals.
- Common schemes include Savings Account, Recurring Deposit (RD), Fixed Deposit (FD), Public Provident Fund (PPF), Senior Citizen Savings Scheme (SCSS) and Monthly Income Scheme (MIS).
- Offer guaranteed returns at rates declared by the government.

- Require low minimum investment amounts and are accessible to all.
- Some schemes, like PPF, provide tax benefits under Section 80C.
- Ideal for secure wealth creation, retirement planning and financial stability.

TRADITIONAL SAVING OPTIONS

These are conventional methods of saving money that offer safety and fixed returns. Common examples include savings accounts, fixed deposits, recurring deposits and post office schemes. (*See Chapter 1 for savings, fixed deposits and recurring deposit details.*)

GOVERNMENT-BACKED SCHEMES

These are saving and investment programmes introduced and supported by the GoI to promote financial security and inclusion among citizens. These schemes are considered safe because they are backed by a sovereign guarantee, often provide fixed returns and may also offer tax benefits. Examples include the PPF, National Savings Certificate (NSC), Sukanya Samriddhi Yojana (SSY) and Senior Citizens Savings Scheme (SCSS).

1. Provident Fund: A Retirement Savings Tool

A PF is a savings scheme where both employees and employers contribute a portion of their salaries, which grows with interest and is paid as a lump sum upon retirement or under specific conditions. While salaried individuals benefit from employer-linked PF schemes, others can also invest in voluntary PF options.

Types of Provident Funds

1. **Employees' Provident Fund (EPF)** – For salaried employees, with contributions from both employer and employee.
2. **Public Provident Fund (PPF)** – Open to all Indian residents, offering long-term, tax-free returns.
3. **General Provident Fund (GPF)** – For government employees.
4. **Unrecognized Provident Fund (URPF)** – Managed by private employers without tax benefits under the EPF Act, 1952.

Key Features of EPF

- **Interest Rate (2024-25):** 8.25 per cent (revised annually by EPFO and the finance ministry).
- **Tax Benefits:** Employer contributions (up to 12 per cent of basic salary + DA) are tax-free. Employee contributions qualify for section 80C deductions, while the maturity amount and interest earned are tax-exempt.
- **Withdrawals:** Allowed after unemployment for more than two months and during the employment period for certain reasons like medical emergencies, home purchase, marriage, etc.
- **Online Management:** The EPF balance can be checked via the EPFO portal, the UMANG app, SMS or missed call service.
- **Universal Account Number (UAN):** Essential for withdrawals and transfers; must be linked with Aadhaar and bank details.
- **Job Change Complications:** Employees should merge old EPF accounts into the current one to avoid multiple UANs. EPFO has simplified transfers via Form-13, eliminating dual approvals (since 2025).
- **Merging EPF Accounts:** Ensures consolidated pension benefits and easier tax-tracking. If an employee has two UANs, the previous one can be deactivated by emailing **uanepf@epfindia.gov.in**.

EPF Account: Activation, UAN, Withdrawals and Common Issues

1. **When an EPF Account Gets Activated:** Your EPF account is activated when your employer registers you with the EPFO and a **UAN** is generated. The UAN remains the same throughout your career and simplifies tracking contributions across employers. If you already have a UAN, your new employer should link it; otherwise, a new UAN is created.

2. **How to Activate UAN and Access Your Account**

   You can activate your UAN online via the EPFO portal to access your PF account, check balances and initiate transfers or withdrawals. As of August 2025, the EPFO allows instant UAN activation through the UMANG mobile app using Face ID, further simplifying the process.

3. **Withdrawing or Transferring EPF**

   You can withdraw your EPF after satisfying conditions such as retirement, job change or emergencies. However, it is recommended to transfer your EPF from your old job to your current one to keep your savings consolidated, help earn optimal interest and ensure smooth account management.

4. **What Happens When a New Employer Opens a Fresh UAN?**

   Sometimes, due to administrative errors, new employers create a fresh UAN instead of linking the existing one. It can cause confusion and difficulty when making withdrawals or transfers. If this happens, it is important to request that the EPFO merge your multiple UANs, ensuring all contributions are consolidated under one account.

5. **Inoperative or Transaction-Less EPF Accounts**

   An EPF account becomes inoperative if there are no contributions or transactions (other than interest) for 36 months or after the member reaches 58 years of age. Although these accounts continue to earn interest, they are subject to enhanced verification before processing withdrawals. If your account is transaction-less and lacks KYC or Aadhaar linking, you may need to visit the EPF field office to update details or activate the account, as standard online processes may not apply.

6. **Blocking and Unblocking Inactive Accounts**

   EPFO's updated Standard Operating Procedure (SOP) imposes restrictions on inoperative accounts, including disabling withdrawals or transfers. To unblock, members need to fulfil KYC requirements and submit a formal request via the member portal or the field office. The unblocking process may take twenty to twenty-five days, depending on verification requirements.

Summary Table

Scenario	Solution/Action
Already have UAN, switching jobs	Ensure new employer links the same UAN
UAN not activated	Activate via EPFO portal or UMANG App using Face ID
Account is transaction-less or inoperative	Visit field office or submit portal request post-KYC
Multiple UANs exist	Request EPFO to merge accounts
Want to withdraw or transfer	Complete KYC, activate UAN, request transfer/withdrawal

2. Public Provident Fund (PPF): A Safe Long-Term Investment

PPF is a government-backed, low-risk savings scheme with tax-free returns.

Key Features of PPF:

- **Tenure:** Minimum fifteen years, extendable in five-years blocks.
- **Investment Limits:** ₹500 to ₹1.5 lakh per year (excess deposits earn no interest).
- **Interest Rate (July–September 2025–26):** 7.1 per cent p.a. (compounded annually, revised quarterly).
- **Tax Benefits:** Contributions are eligible for deduction under Section 80C and tax-free interest and maturity amount.
- **Deposit Rules:** A minimum of one deposit is required each year. Deposits made after the fifth day of the month do not earn interest for that month.
- **Withdrawal and loan:** Partial withdrawals are allowed after six years; loans are available after three years.

- **Nomination:** Permitted at account opening or later.
- **Where to Open:** Available at banks and post offices.

3. General Provident Fund (GPF) for Government Employees

The GPF, established in the year 1960, is a retirement savings scheme exclusively for government employees, railway staff and employees of recognized educational institutions. Private-sector employees are not eligible for this scheme.

Key Features of GPF:

- **Interest Rate:** Revised periodically by the government (currently 7.1 per cent p.a. for July–September 2025-26).
- **Tax Implications:**
  - If an employee's annual contribution exceeds ₹2.5 lakh, the interest earned on the excess amount is taxable.
  - If the employer does not contribute, the tax-free limit increases to ₹5 lakh.
  - Contributions are eligible for deduction under Section 80C and the maturity amount is tax-free.
- Withdrawals: Permitted for specific needs, but excessive withdrawals may impact the retirement corpus.

4. Unrecognized Provident Fund (URPF)

Under the EPF Act, 1952, organizations with more than 20 employees must either join the EPFO scheme or set up an independent PF trust approved by the income tax commissioner.

- **Recognized PF:** Offers tax benefits on contributions, interest and withdrawals.
- **Unrecognized PF (URPF):** If the commissioner does not approve of the trust, the scheme becomes unrecognized, resulting in the loss of tax exemptions.
  - Employer contributions are taxable as salary income.
  - Interest earned is taxable under *Income from Other Sources.*
  - Lump sum withdrawal is tax-free, but annuity payments are taxable.

5. National Savings Certificate (NSC)

The Certificate is a fixed-income savings scheme offered by the Government of India through post offices. It is a secure investment option, primarily designed for small and middle-income investors who want guaranteed returns along with tax benefits.

Key Features:

- **Issuer:** Government of India (through post offices).
- **Eligibility:** Only Indian residents can invest. NRIs are not allowed.
- **Minimum Investment:** ₹1,000 (in multiples of ₹100). There is no maximum limit.
- **Tenure:** 5 years (fixed).
- **Interest Rate:** Fixed and announced by the government every quarter. Interest is compounded annually but payable at maturity.
- **Mode of Holding:** Can be purchased in single name, joint name or on behalf of a minor.
- **Premature Withdrawal:** Not permitted, except under specific conditions such as the death of the holder or court order.

Tax Benefits:

- **Section 80C Deduction:** Investment in NSC is eligible for tax deduction under Section 80C of the Income Tax Act, up to ₹1.5 lakh per financial year.
- **Interest Tax Treatment:** The interest earned is taxable, but each year's interest (except the final year) is considered reinvested and qualifies for deduction under Section 80C.

Additional Details:

- NSCs can be used as collateral security to avail loans from banks and NBFCs.
- A safe option for risk-averse investors as it carries a sovereign guarantee.
- Available only at post offices (not banks).

6. Sukanya Samriddhi Yojana (SSY)

The Sukanya Yojana is a small savings scheme launched by the Government of India under the *Beti Bachao Beti Padhao* campaign. It is specially designed to encourage savings for the education and marriage expenses of a girl child. The scheme provides attractive interest rates and tax benefits, making it one of the most preferred long-term savings options for parents.

Key Features:

- **Eligibility:** A parent or legal guardian can open an account in the name of a girl child below 10 years of age.
- **Number of Accounts:** Only one account per girl child and a maximum of two accounts in a family (exceptions for twins or triplets).
- **Minimum Investment:** ₹250 per year.
- **Maximum Investment:** ₹1.5 lakh per year.
- **Tenure:** 21 years from the date of account opening or until the girl child's marriage after 18 years of age.
- **Deposit Period:** Deposits can be made for 15 years; after that, the account continues to earn interest until maturity.
- **Interest Rate:** Decided quarterly by the government. Interest is compounded annually and credited to the account.
- **Withdrawal:** A partial withdrawal of up to 50 per cent of the balance is allowed when the girl reaches 18 years of age, for higher education or marriage.
- **Premature Closure:** Permitted in cases of marriage after 18 years, death of the account holder or medical emergencies (under specific conditions).

Tax Benefits:

- **Section 80C Deduction:** Deposits are eligible for deduction under Section 80C of the Income Tax Act, up to ₹1.5 lakh per year.
- **EEE Status:** SSY enjoys Exempt-Exempt-Exempt status:

1. Investment is tax-deductible.

2. Interest earned is tax-free.
3. The amount at maturity is also tax-free.

Additional Details:

- The account can be transferred anywhere in India if the guardian shifts residence.
- Operated through both post offices and authorized banks.
- Provides financial security for a girl child with government-backed assurance.

7. Senior Citizens Savings Scheme (SCSS)

The SCSS is a government-backed savings scheme designed to provide financial security and a regular income to senior citizens. It is one of the safest and most popular investment options for retirees offering assured returns and tax benefits.

Key Features:

- **Eligibility:**
  - Indian citizens aged 60 years or above.
  - Retired individuals aged 55-60 years who have opted for voluntary retirement/superannuation can also invest, provided they do so within 1 month of receiving their retirement benefits.
- **Minimum Investment:** ₹1,000.
- **Maximum Investment:** ₹30 lakh (individually or jointly).
- **Tenure:** Five years (can be extended for three more years after maturity).
- **Interest Rate:** Fixed and announced by the government every quarter. Interest is paid quarterly.
- **Premature Withdrawal:** Allowed after one year with penalty charges (1.5 per cent deduction if closed after one year, one per cent deduction if closed after two years).

Tax Benefits:

- **Section 80C Deduction:** Investments are eligible for deduction under Section 80C of the Income Tax Act, up to ₹1.5 lakh per year.

- **Tax on Interest:** Interest earned is fully taxable as per the investor's tax slab.
- **TDS:** If annual interest exceeds ₹50,000, TDS (Tax Deducted at Source) is applicable.

Additional Details:

- An account can be opened in a single name or jointly with a spouse.
- Provides a steady quarterly income, making it ideal for retirees.
- Available through post offices and authorized banks across India.
- Carrying a sovereign guarantee, it is considered a very safe option for senior citizens.

8. Atal Pension Yojana (APY) for the Unorganized Sector

There is a government-backed pension scheme aimed at workers in the unorganized sector. It aims to ensure that individuals have a fixed monthly pension after retirement, thereby promoting financial stability in old age.

Key Features:

- **Eligibility:**
  - Any Indian citizen aged 18 to 40 years.
  - Must have a savings bank account.
- **Contribution Period:** A minimum of 20 years (until the subscriber turns 60).
- **Pension Amount:** Guaranteed fixed pension ranging from ₹1,000 to ₹5,000 per month, depending on the contribution made and the age of joining.
- **Government Contribution:** For eligible subscribers (who joined between 2015-2016 and were not income-tax payers or covered under other social security schemes), the government co-contributed 50 per cent of the total contribution or ₹1,000 per year, whichever is lower, for five years.
- **Pension Start:** Pension begins at 60 years of age.

- **Spouse Benefit:** After the subscriber's death, the spouse is entitled to receive the pension. After the spouse's death, the nominee gets the accumulated corpus.
- **Premature Exit:** Exit is not allowed before 60 years, except in cases of death or terminal illness.

Tax Benefits:

- Contributions to APY qualify for a deduction under section 80CCD (1) up to ₹1.5 lakh.
- Additional deduction of up to ₹50,000 is available under section 80CCD (1B) (same as National Pension System).

Additional Details:

- Administered by the Pension Fund Regulatory and Development Authority (PFRDA).
- Automatic debit facility ensures timely contributions.
- Designed especially for workers in the unorganized sector, such as maids, drivers, labourers, gardeners, etc.
- Provides a safety net in retirement with a guaranteed pension backed by the Government of India.

9. Pradhan Mantri Jan Dhan Yojana (PMJDY)

The PMJDY is a flagship financial inclusion programme launched by the Government of India in August 2014. Its main objective is to ensure access to financial services such as banking, savings, credit, insurance and pension facilities for all households, especially those in rural and economically weaker sections of society.

Key Features:

- **Eligibility:** Available to all Indian citizens aged 10 years and above.
- **Zero-Balance Account:** Accounts can be opened with no minimum balance requirement.
- **Account Type:** Basic Savings Bank Deposit Account (BSBDA) that offers simple banking facilities.
- **Accidental Insurance Cover:** Free accidental insurance cover of up to ₹2 lakh for account holders (linked with RuPay debit card).

- **Life Insurance Cover:** One-time life insurance cover of ₹30,000 (conditions apply, for accounts opened within the specified time).
- **Overdraft Facility:** Overdraft facility of up to ₹10,000 after six months of satisfactory account operation, preferably to the woman head of the household.
- **Direct Benefit Transfer (DBT):** Government subsidies and benefits can be directly credited to the beneficiary's account. It aims to reduce delays, eliminate middlemen and improve transparency in welfare schemes like LPG subsidies, scholarships and pension payments.
- **Mobile Banking & RuPay Card:** Provides a RuPay debit card for easy digital transactions.
- **Interest on Deposits:** Savings in the account earn interest, just like a traditional savings bank account.

Tax Benefits:

- No direct tax deduction is available under PMJDY.
- However, money saved in the account earns interest, which is taxable according to income tax rules.

- PMJDY is considered the world's largest financial inclusion scheme, bringing millions of previously unbanked individuals into the formal banking system.

4. MARKET-LINKED INVESTMENTS

These are financial products whose returns are directly linked to the performance of market instruments such as equities, bonds, indices or other securities. Unlike fixed-return investments (like FDs or PPF) that provide assured interest, the returns in market-linked investments vary, depending on market movements. Some of the market-linked investments are:

1. Shares / Equities

Shares (also called equities) represent ownership in a company. When an investor buys shares of a company, they become a part-owner (shareholder) of that company. They are entitled to a portion of its profits as well as voting rights in certain company decisions.

Key Features:

- **Ownership:** Shares give the investor part-ownership in the company.
- **Returns:** Investors can earn through

1. **Dividends** – a share of the company's profits distributed to shareholders.
2. **Capital Gains** – profit from selling shares at a higher price than the purchase price.

- Types of Shares:

1. **Equity Shares** – carry voting rights and represent ownership.
2. **Preference Shares** – give priority in receiving dividends and repayment at the time of winding up, but usually have limited or no voting rights.

- **Liquidity:** Shares of listed companies can be easily bought or sold on stock exchanges such as NSE or BSE in India.
- **Risk and Reward:** High return potential but also high risk due to market fluctuations.
- **Divisibility:** Investors can buy even a small number of shares, depending on their affordability.

2. Mutual Funds

A mutual fund is a type of investment scheme where money from many investors is pooled together and invested in a diversified portfolio of securities such as shares, bonds, government securities or money market instruments. These funds are managed by professional fund managers on behalf of investors.

Key Features:

- **Pooling of Funds:** Collects money from multiple investors.

- **Professional Management:** Investments are managed by qualified fund managers.
- **Diversification:** Reduces risk by investing across different sectors and asset classes.
- **Liquidity:** Units of most mutual funds (except ELSS and close-ended funds) can be redeemed at any time.
- **Net Asset Value (NAV):** The value of each mutual fund unit is based on the NAV, which fluctuates daily in response to market performance.
- **Accessibility:** Even small investors can start investing, with as little as ₹500–₹1,000.

Types of Mutual Funds:

- **Equity Funds** – Invest mainly in shares, higher risk but higher return potential.
- **Debt Funds** – Invest in bonds and fixed-income securities, offering safer but lower returns.
- **Hybrid Funds** – Mix of equity and debt, balancing risk and return.
- **Equity Linked Savings Scheme (ELSS)** – Equity-based funds that also provide tax benefits.

Tax Benefits:

- Investment in ELSS funds qualifies for tax exemption under section 80C up to ₹1.5 lakh per year, under Section 80C of the Income Tax Act.
- Tax on gains depends on the type of fund and holding period (STCG vs LTCG rules apply).

3. Exchange Traded Funds (ETFs)

An ETF is a type of investment fund that pools money from investors and invests in a basket of securities. Unlike mutual funds, ETFs are traded on stock exchanges just like individual shares, making them easy to buy and sell throughout the trading day.

Key Features:

- **Trading on Exchange:** ETFs can be bought and sold on stock

exchanges (like NSE and BSE) at market prices during trading hours.

- **Diversification:** Each ETF represents a diversified basket of securities, helping to spread risk.

Types of ETFs:

  - **Equity ETFs** – track stock indices, such as the Nifty 50 or Sensex.
  - **Debt ETFs** – invest in bonds and government securities.
  - **Commodity ETFs** – invest in commodities like gold (e.g., gold ETFs).
  - **International ETFs** – track global indices or foreign markets.

- **Liquidity:** High liquidity, as they are exchange-traded.
- **Transparency:** Holdings of ETFs are usually disclosed daily.
- **Low Costs:** Generally, they have lower expense ratios than actively managed mutual funds.
- **NAV vs. Market Price:** Unlike mutual funds (bought at NAV), ETFs are purchased at the market price, which may be slightly above or below the NAV.

Tax Treatment:

- **Equity ETFs:** Taxed like equity shares (STCG @15 per cent, LTCG @10 per cent beyond ₹1 lakh if held over 12 months).
- **Debt/Gold ETFs:** Taxed like debt funds (STCG as per slab, LTCG @20 per cent with indexation after three years).

4. Gold Investments

It refers to the purchase of gold in various forms with the aim of wealth preservation, diversification and hedging against inflation. Gold is considered a safe-haven asset, meaning it usually retains or increases its value during times of economic uncertainty.

Key Features:

- **Forms of Investment:**
  - **Physical Gold** – jewellery, coins, bars (traditional but comes with making charges and storage issues).

- **Gold Exchange Traded Funds (ETFs)** – units that represent physical gold, traded on stock exchanges.
- **Sovereign Gold Bonds (SGBs)** – government securities denominated in grams of gold, offering interest plus price appreciation.
- **Gold Mutual Funds** – invest in Gold ETFs on behalf of investors.
- **Digital Gold** – bought online through apps, stored in insured vaults by the provider.

- **Liquidity:** Gold is highly liquid and can be easily sold in the market.
- **Safety:** Government-backed products like SGBs are safer compared to physical gold.
- **Returns:** Depend on global gold prices; does not provide regular income like interest or dividends (except SGBs, which pay 2.5 per cent interest annually).

Tax Treatment:

- **Physical Gold / Gold ETFs / Gold Funds:**
  - STCG (if sold within 3 years) – taxed as per the income tax slab.
  - LTCG (if sold after 3 years) – taxed at 20 per cent with indexation benefit.
- **Sovereign Gold Bonds (SGBs):**
  - Interest earned (2.5 per cent p.a.) is taxable.
  - **Capital gains on redemption at maturity are tax-free** (a major benefit).

5. Real Estate Investment

Real estate is a tangible, high-return asset class with long-term appreciation potential. It is best for investors with substantial funds, seeking long-term wealth growth.

- Gold is considered a hedge against inflation and currency fluctuations.
- Acts as a diversifier in an investment portfolio to reduce overall risk.
- However, gold does not generate productive income like businesses or fixed deposits; returns mainly depend on market price movement.

Key Features:

- **Capital Appreciation:** Property values typically rise over time.
- **Rental Income:** Provides steady cash flow.
- **Low Volatility:** More stable compared to stocks.
- **High Entry Cost:** Requires significant initial capital.

5. Retirement Planning Options

Retirement Planning Options are financial tools and schemes designed to help individuals build a secure income for their post-retirement life. They include government-backed pensions, provident funds, insurance-based plans, and market-linked investments to ensure financial independence in old age.

1. Pension Planning for Retirement

Beyond PF, pension schemes ensure a steady income during post-retirement life. A pension provides a regular income post-retirement, ensuring financial independence.

Key Aspects of Being a Pensioner:

1. **Pension Disbursement:** It can be received through banks (no separate account required) or post offices.
2. **Account Transfer:** Pension accounts can be shifted between banks/ branches.
3. **Life Certificate Submission:** It must be submitted annually in November, either by visiting a bank branch or through Jeevan Pramaan (an Aadhaar-based digital verification).

Retirement Planning Strategies

1. **Start Early:** Starting at age 25 allows for 35 years of compounding, assuming a retirement age of sixty.
2. **Medical and Emergency Fund:** Allocate savings for healthcare and emergencies.
3. **Children's Future:** Balance retirement savings with education/ marriage expenses.
4. **Regular Review:** Monitor investments for liquidity, risk and returns.
5. **Avoid Premature Withdrawals:** Preserve retirement corpus by limiting unnecessary spending.

2. Unified Pension Scheme (UPS)

Eligibility:

- Existing central government employees enrolled under NPS as of 1 April 2025.
- New recruits joining the central government service on or after 1 April 2025. Deadline for them is 30 September 2025.
- Retired NPS subscribers (superannuated, voluntary retirement or under FR 56(j)) on or before 30 September 2025.
- Legally wedded spouses of deceased NPS subscribers who passed away before choosing UPS

Key Benefits:

- **Guaranteed Pension:** *50 per cent of last 12 months' basic pay (a minimum of ₹10,000/month).*
- **Family Pension:** 60 per cent of the pension to spouse after death.
- **Inflation-Adjusted:** Protects against rising costs.

3. National Pension System (NPS)

- **Open to All:** Includes private employees, self-employed and NRIs.
- **Market-Linked Returns:** Invests in equities, bonds and government securities.

Withdrawal Rules:

- 60 per cent lump sum (tax-free).
- 40 per cent used to buy an annuity (taxable).
- **Risk vs. Reward:** Higher potential returns but no guaranteed pension.

Who Should Choose What?

- UPS: Ideal for risk-averse government employees seeking stability. Private employees can't apply.
- NPS: Best for those with market knowledge and long-term horizon.

Distinguish between UPS and NPS

Features	Unified Pension Scheme (UPS)	National Pension System (NPS)
Launch	Effective from 1 April 2025	Introduced in 2004 for govt. employees, later extended to all citizens
Eligibility	Govt. employees (existing & new), retired NPS subscribers (till 30 September 2025) and spouses of deceased NPS subscribers	Open to all Indian citizens (18–70 years)
Nature of Benefit	**Defined Benefit** - Assured pension after retirement	**Defined Contribution** – Pension depends on market returns and annuity purchase

Features	Unified Pension Scheme (UPS)	National Pension System (NPS)
Employee Contribution	10 per cent of basic pay + DA	10 per cent of basic pay + DA (for govt. employees)
Government Contribution	14 per cent of basic pay + DA	14 per cent of basic pay + DA (for govt. employees)
Pension Guarantee	Guaranteed pension of 50 per cent of last drawn salary (basic + DA)	No guarantee – pension depends on accumulated corpus and annuity rates
Retirement Benefits	Pension + family pension	Pension based on annuity + lump sum withdrawal (up to 60 per cent)
Tax Treatment	To be notified (likely similar to NPS exemptions under 80C/80CCD)	Contributions eligible under Sec 80CCD (1) and 80CCD (1B) (up to ₹2 lakh)

Features	Unified Pension Scheme (UPS)	National Pension System (NPS)
Risk Factor	Low – Govt. assured	14 per cent of basic pay + DA (for govt. employees)
Portability	Available only to central govt. employees	No guarantee – pension depends on accumulated corpus and annuity rates
Choice Deadline	Existing employees & retirees: 30 Sep 2025; New recruits: within 30 days of joining	Pension based on annuity + lump sum withdrawal (up to 60 per cent)

6. INSURANCE AS INVESTMENT-CUM-PROTECTION

Insurance is a financial safety net that protects individuals and businesses from unexpected losses due to accidents, illnesses, theft or natural disasters. It works as a contract (policy) between the policyholder (buyer) and the insurer (company), where the insurer agrees to compensate for covered losses in exchange for getting a premium paid by the policyholder.

Why is Insurance Important?

- **Financial Security:** Covers high-cost damages (e.g., medical bills, car repairs).

- **Risk Management:** Transfers financial risk from the individual to the insurer.
- **Legal Requirement:** Some insurances (e.g., motor insurance) are mandatory.
- **Peace of Mind:** Ensures protection for loved ones and valuable assets.

Risk vs. Protection

- **Risk:** Potential for financial loss (e.g., accidents, illnesses, theft).
- **Protection:** Insurance acts as a shield, covering losses so you do not bear the full cost. Sometimes it is almost equal.

Type of Risk	Insurance Protection
Car accident	Motor Insurance
Critical illness	Health Insurance
Home damage	Home/Property Insurance
Death of breadwinner	Life Insurance
Travel emergencies	Travel Insurance

What can you Insure?

Insurance helps protect you financially from unexpected losses. You can insure various aspects of your life, such as:

1. Protecting your Assets

- **Car Insurance:** Covers accidents, theft and third-party liabilities.
- **Home Insurance:** Protects against fire, natural disasters and burglary.
- **Gadget Insurance:** Covers phones, laptops and other electronics.

2. Protecting your Health and Life

- **Health Insurance:** Pays for hospitalizations, surgeries and medications.

- **Life Insurance:** Provides a lump sum to the family after the policyholder's death.
- **Term Insurance:** Pure life cover with no maturity benefits (low premium).

3. Protecting Income and Liabilities

- **Income Protection:** Replaces lost income due to disability/job loss.
- **Critical Illness Insurance:** Covers diseases like cancer/heart attacks.

Key Components of an Insurance Policy

An insurance policy consists of essential elements like premium, coverage, exclusions, policy term and claim process, which define your rights and responsibilities as a policyholder.

1. Premium

- The cost you pay (monthly/annually) to keep the policy active.
- **Factors affecting premium:**
  - **Auto Insurance:** Driving history, car model, age of vehicle, etc.
  - **Health Insurance:** Age, pre-existing conditions, coverage.
  - **Life Insurance:** Age, health, smoking habits.

2. Policy Limit

- The maximum amount the insurer will pay for a claim.
  - Per incident (e.g., ₹5 lakh for car repairs).
  - Lifetime limit (e.g., ₹50 lakh in health insurance).

3. Deductible

- The out-of-pocket amount you pay before the insurer covers the rest.
  - Example: If your health insurance has a ₹10,000 deductible, you pay the first ₹10,000 of medical bills, then the insurance company reimburses that amount.

Types of Insurance Policies

Insurance Type	Coverage	Best For
Term Life Insurance	Death benefit (no maturity value)	Young earners, family providers
Health Insurance	Hospitalization, surgeries, medicines	Everyone (individual/ family)
Motor Insurance	Accidents, theft, third-party damage	Car/bike owners
Home Insurance	Fire, burglary, natural disasters	Homeowners/renters
Travel Insurance	Flight cancellations, medical emergencies	Frequent travellers
Group Insurance	Employer-provided (life/health)	Corporate employees/ any group or association

Generally, the term insurance cannot give any maturity benefit. However, now, some term insurances are providing maturity benefit too. They are not standard pure term policy. Those are term plan with return of premium (TROP) option. So all premiums will be refunded if you survive the entire policy term of such plan.

Additional Insurance Features

1. Riders and Top-up Plans

- **Riders:** Add-ons (e.g., critical illness cover in a life insurance policy).
- **Top-Up Plans:** Extra coverage beyond base policy limits.

2. Floater Policies

- Covers multiple family members under one plan (e.g., family health insurance).

3. Portability

- Allows switching insurers without losing benefits (common in health insurance).

Types of Insurance and Their Purpose

Insurance acts as a financial shield, protecting individuals and businesses from unexpected losses. Broadly, insurance falls into two categories:

1. **Life Insurance** – Covers risks related to human life (death, disability).
2. **General Insurance** – Covers non-life assets (health, vehicles, property, travel).

1. Life Insurance

Purpose:

- Provides financial security to the insured's family in case of premature death or permanent disability.
- Offers survival benefits if the policyholder outlives the term.

Types of Life Insurance

Tax Benefits:

- Premiums qualify for the Section 80C deduction.
- Maturity/death benefits are tax-free under section 10 (10D).

HEALTH INSURANCE

Why It's Essential?

- Rising medical care cost inflation makes treatments unaffordable.
- Covers hospitalization, surgeries and critical illnesses.

Key Features:

- Cashless hospitalization at network hospitals
- Coverage of pre- and post-hospitalization expenses
- Tax benefits available under the section 80D

Types of Health Insurance

- Individual Health Insurance (Covers one person).
- Family Floater Policy (Single policy for entire family).
- Critical Illness Cover (Lump sum payout for diseases like cancer).
- Senior Citizen Plans (Tailored for ages above 60).

Check Before Buying:

- Waiting periods for pre-existing diseases.
- Sub-limits (e.g., room-rent capping).

3. Home/Property Insurance

What's Covered?

- Structural damage (fire, floods, earthquakes).
- Theft and burglary of valuables (jewellery, gadgets).
- Third-party liability (e.g., visitor injury in your home).

Who Needs It?

Type	Key Features	Best For
Term Insurance	- Pure life cover (no maturity benefit) - Low premium, high coverage	Young earners, family providers
Whole Life Policy	- Covers entire lifetime - Pays death benefit + sometimes maturity bonus	Long-term wealth protection
Endowment Plans	- Life cover + savings - Pays lump sum on maturity/death	Risk-averse savers
Unit Linked Insurance Plans (ULIPs)	- Combines insurance + market-linked investments - Potential for higher returns	Investors seeking growth + coverage
Pension Plans	- Regular income post-retirement - Options: Immediate or deferred annuity	Retirement planning

- Homeowners
- Tenant/Renters (for personal belongings)

4. Motor Insurance (Auto/Vehicle Insurance)

Types of Motor Insurance (Mandatory as per Motor Vehicles Act, 1988)

1. Third-Party Insurance (Covers damage/injury to others).
2. Comprehensive Insurance (Covers own vehicle + third-party).

Key Benefits:

- Accidental repairs/replacement.
- Personal accident covers for the owner-driver.
- Theft protection.

5. Travel Insurance

It covers:

- Trip cancellations/delays.
- Medical emergencies abroad.
- Lost baggage/passport.

Best For:

- International travellers.
- Frequent flyers.

6 Group Insurance

It can give competitive premium rates if you are a member of certain groups (employer-employee group or non-employer-employee group). Group insurance can offer life or health insurance. Examples of such groups: holder of the same credit card, member of some association.

How It Works?

- Offered by employers, banks or associations.
- Covers life, health or accident risks.

Advantages and Limitations

Advantages	Limitations
Lower premiums	Coverage ends if you leave the group
No medical tests	Limited customization

1. Top-up and Rider Plans

Top-up Health Insurance

- Extends coverage when base policy exhausts (e.g., ₹5 lakh base + ₹5 lakh top-up).

Riders (Add-ons)

- Critical Illness Rider (Lump sum on diagnosis).
- Accidental Death Rider (Extra payout for accidents).

2. Floater Policies

What Is It?

- Single policy covering multiple family members/items (e.g., health, jewellery).

Pros:

- Cost-effective (cheaper than individual policies).
- Flexible coverage.

Cons:

- Shared sum insured (if one member claims heavily, others get less).
- The premium is based on the oldest member's age, so younger member has to pay a relatively high premium.

ALTERNATIVE AND EMERGING INVESTMENT OPTIONS

Alternative and emerging investment options refer to non-traditional avenues of investing that extend beyond conventional assets like fixed deposits, savings accounts or regular equity and debt instruments. These options are gaining popularity among investors seeking higher returns, diversification and exposure to new markets or asset classes. For example:

1. Real Estate Investment Trusts (REITs)

REITs allow investment in real estate without the need to directly own properties. They generate income through rent or property appreciation. REITs are suitable for those wanting exposure to real estate without the hassles of property management.

Key Features:

- **Dividend Income:** Regular payouts from rental earnings.
- **Accessibility:** Both small and large investors can participate.
- **Liquidity:** Traded on stock exchanges like equities.
- **No Tax Benefits:** Market-linked, hence taxable.

2. Government Bonds

Government bonds (or sovereign bonds) are low-risk debt securities issued by the central or state governments to fund public projects. It is ideal for conservative investors prioritizing capital preservation and steady income.

Key Features:

- **Risk-Free:** Backed by the government, ensuring high safety of principal.
- **Liquidity:** Tradable in secondary markets for easy exit.
- **Tax Benefits:** No TDS on interest; some bonds (like tax-free bonds) offer exemptions.
- **Flexible Tenures:** Range from 5 to 40 years.
- **Types Include:**
  - Fixed-rate bonds (steady interest).
  - Floating-rate bonds (interest adjusts with market rates).
  - Inflation-indexed bonds (protect against rising prices).

3. RBI Bonds

RBI Bonds are fixed-income securities issued by the RBI, offering semi-annual interest payouts. These bonds are suitable for conservative investors looking for secure, government-backed returns.

Key Features:

- **Interest Rate:** 8.05 per cent p.a. (subject to change).
- **Tenure:** Seven years, with premature redemption only for senior citizens.
- **Taxation:** Interest is taxable under the Income Tax Act, 1961.
- **Investment Mode:** Electronic form (bond ledger account).

- **No Wealth Tax:** Returns are exempt from wealth tax.

4. Corporate Bonds

Corporate bonds are debt instruments issued by companies to raise capital for business expansion, infrastructure development or other financial needs. Investors lend money to corporations in exchange for periodic interest payments and the return of principal upon maturity. It is ideal for investors seeking higher returns than FDs with moderate risk tolerance.

Key Features:

- **Fixed Incomes:** Provide regular interest payments, making it suitable for stable income seekers.
- **Credit Ratings:** Agencies like CRISIL and ICRA assess the safety of bonds; higher ratings (AAA, AA) indicate lower default risk.
- **Maturity Periods:** Range from short-term (1–5 years) to long-term (10 years or more).
- **Higher Returns Than FDs:** Offer better yields than bank's FD but carries relatively higher risk.
- **Capital Appreciation Potential:** Bond prices may rise if interest rates fall or the issuer's creditworthiness improves.
- **Market Risks:** Sensitive to economic conditions, interest rate changes and sector-specific downturns.

5. Debentures

Debentures are long-term debt instruments issued by companies or

> - Credit ratings help investors assess the safety of financial products like bonds and fixed deposits. Agencies such as **CRISIL**, **ICRA** *and* **CARE** *evaluate a company's ability to repay its debt.*
> - Higher ratings (like AAA) indicate lower risk, while lower ratings (like BB or below) suggest higher risk. Always check the credit rating before investing in company deposits or bonds.

- **Credit Rating Information Services of India Limited (CRISIL)**
  CRISIL is India's first and largest credit rating agency. It evaluates the creditworthiness of companies, financial institutions and debt instruments, helping investors make informed decisions.
- **Investment Information and Credit Rating Agency (ICRA)**
  ICRA is a well-known Indian credit rating agency that assigns ratings to corporate bonds, fixed deposits and commercial papers. It provides research and risk analysis to support investment choices.
- **Credit Analysis and Research Limited (CARE)**
  CARE Ratings offers credit ratings for a wide range of debt instruments and companies. It helps assess the risk level associated with lending or investing in specific entities.

governments to raise capital. Investors should check credit ratings before investing to assess the risk levels associated with their investments.

Key Features:

- **Fixed Returns:** Offer periodic interest payments.
- **Maturity Period:** Have a predefined repayment date.
- **Security:** Can be secured (backed by assets) or unsecured (higher risk, higher returns).
- **Transferability:** Tradable in secondary markets for liquidity.
- **Types:** Convertible (can be turned into equity) and non-convertible (fixed returns).

6. Cryptocurrencies

Digital assets like Bitcoin and Ethereum operate on decentralized blockchain networks, offering high volatility and speculative returns. It is ideal for aggressive investors who are comfortable with high risk and market uncertainty.

Key Features:

- **High Risk/Reward:** Extreme price swings; potential for significant gains/losses.
- **Taxation:** Profits are taxed at 30 per cent, along with 1 per cent TDS on each transaction in India.

- **Unregulated:** No central authority oversight; requires vigilant research.

8. RISK, RETURN AND LIQUIDITY COMPARISON

It is the process of evaluating different investment options by analyzing three key aspects:

1. **Risk** – the possibility of losing part or all of the invested money or the uncertainty of expected returns. For example, equities carry higher risk while government bonds are low-risk.
2. **Return** – the profit or gain generated from an investment that can be in the form of interest, dividends or capital appreciation. Generally, higher returns are linked with higher risks.
3. **Liquidity** – how quickly and easily an investment can be converted into cash without significant loss of value. For instance, savings accounts are highly liquid, while real estate is less liquid.

1. Risk and Return in Investments

Every financial product comes with its own balance of risk and return. Understanding this relationship helps in making informed decisions.

- **Savings accounts** are low-risk, offering easy access to funds, but returns are often minimal and may not outpace inflation.
- **Stocks** are more volatile but can deliver higher returns over the long term, making them suitable for risk-tolerant investors.

The **risk-return trade-off** principle states that the potential of higher returns come with increased risk. Factors like an investor's risk tolerance, time horizon and financial goals influence this balance. For instance, long-term investors can afford to take on higher risks, as they have time to recover from market downturns, whereas short-term investors may prefer stability.

Types of Investment Risks

1. **Market (Systematic) Risk** – Affects the entire market due to economic, political or global factors (e.g., recessions, stock market crashes).
2. **Unsystematic Risk** – Specific to a company or industry (e.g., management changes, product recalls).

3. **Inflation Risk** – The danger that rising prices erode purchasing power over time.
4. **Liquidity Risk** – Difficulty in selling an investment quickly without significant loss.
5. **Business Risk** – The possibility of a company underperforming or failing.
6. **Volatility Risk** – Price fluctuations in investments, even if the underlying business is stable.
7. **Currency Risk** – Losses due to unfavourable exchange rate movements in foreign investments.

2. Discussion on Different Saving and Investment Options

A recession is a period of significant economic decline, usually lasting for at least two consecutive quarters. It is marked by reduced consumer spending, job losses, falling incomes, lower industrial production, affecting investments and business profits.

For example: The world faced a major recession during the Global Financial Crisis of 2008, which started with the collapse of large financial institutions in the United States. It caused millions of job losses and a sharp decline in stock markets across the world.

Saving and investment options come in various forms, each designed to suit different financial goals, risk levels and time horizons. From traditional schemes like fixed deposits (FD) and post office savings to modern tools such as mutual funds and digital assets, understanding the features and benefits of each option can help individuals make informed financial decisions. This section highlights some popular and accessible choices available in India.

1. Unit Linked Insurance Plan (ULIP)

ULIPs combine insurance coverage with investment opportunities, making them suitable for long-term financial goals such as retirement, education or buying a home.

Key Features:

- **Dual Benefit:** Provides life insurance while investing in equity or debt funds.
- **Flexible Investments:** Choice of funds based on risk appetite (equity, debt or hybrid).
- **Fund Switching Option:** Allows shifting investments between funds based on market conditions.
- **Partial Withdrawals:** Permitted after a five-year lock-in period.
- **Tax Benefits:** Premiums up to ₹1.5 lakh qualify for tax deductions under section 80C and maturity proceeds are tax-free under section 10 (10D).

2. Post Office Monthly Income Scheme (POMIS)

POMIS is a government-backed savings scheme offering fixed monthly returns, making it a low-risk investment option. It is ideal for risk-averse investors seeking a stable monthly income.

Key Features:

- **Eligibility:** Individuals, joint account holders (up to three), minors and guardians can invest.
- **Investment Range:** Minimum ₹1,000 and maximum ₹9 lakh (single) or ₹15 lakh (joint).
- **Interest Rate:** For the first quarter of 2025–26, the interest rate is 7.4 per cent p.a., paid monthly and taxable. However, this rate is not fixed; it is reviewed and may change every quarter.
- **Withdrawal:** This account can be closed five years after it is opened, but withdrawals are not permitted within the first year. In case of premature withdrawal, a penalty (2 per cent deduction if withdrawn within three years, 1 per cent after three years) is charged.

3. Bank Fixed Deposits (FDs)

Bank FDs are secure, fixed-return investments where funds are locked in for a predetermined period at a guaranteed interest rate. Generally, a penalty is charged for premature withdrawal. It is ideal for risk-averse individuals needing predictable returns.

Key Features:

- **Safety:** Insured up to ₹5 lakh per depositor per bank (DICGC coverage).
- **Flexible Tenures:** From 7 days to 10 years.
- **Interest Payout Options:** Cumulative (compounded) or non-cumulative (monthly/quarterly payouts).
- **Senior Citizen Benefits:** Extra 0.25–0.75 per cent interest.
- **Taxation:** No TDS deducted if interest up to ₹50,000/year (₹1 lakh for senior citizens).

4. Company Fixed Deposits

Corporate FDs are term deposits offered by NBFCs and companies,

> The Deposit Insurance and Credit Guarantee Corporation (DICGC) protects your bank deposits in case the bank fails. It insures up to ₹5 lakh per depositor per bank, covering savings, fixed, current and recurring deposits.
>
> **Top Tip:** If you have more than ₹5 lakh, consider spreading it across different banks to stay fully insured.

yielding higher interest than bank FDs but with elevated risk. It is ideal for investors who are comfortable with moderate risk for better returns.

Key Features:

- **Higher Returns:** Rates often surpass bank FDs.
- **Credit Rating Dependency:** opt for AAA/AA-rated companies to minimize default risk.
- **No Insurance:** Not covered under DICGC; so, need research for issuer credibility.

- **Taxation:** TDS applies on interest over ₹5,000/year (avoidable via Form 15G/H).

5. Kisan Vikas Patra (KVP)

A government-backed small savings scheme that doubles investments

Form 15G (for individuals below 60) and **Form 15H** (for senior citizens) are self-declaration forms submitted to the bank to avoid TDS on interest income. You can submit these forms if your total income is below the taxable limit and you do not have any tax liability for the year.

Top Tip: Submit at the start of the financial year to avoid unnecessary TDS deductions.

in 115 months (9 years and 7 months) as of the first quarter of 2025–26, which signifies an interest rate of 7.5 per cent compounded annually. The interest rate is changeable as it is reviewed quarterly. It is ideal for long-term savers seeking secure, doubling investments.

- **No Maximum Limit:** Invest any amount; minimum ₹1,000.
- **Liquidity:** Premature withdrawal allowed after 2.5 years (penalty applies).
- **Transfer and Nomination Facility:** Joint depositor and nomination are available. It is also transferable to the legal heirs in case of the depositor's death.

COMMON MISTAKES TO AVOID

1. **Investing without clear goals** – Putting money into schemes without defining short-term or long-term objectives can lead to poor financial decisions.
2. **Following rumours and herd mentality** – Blindly copying others' investment choices or acting on market rumours often results in losses.

3. **Ignoring risk profile** – Not assessing one's own ability to take risks may lead to investments that are either too risky or too conservative.
4. **Lack of emergency fund** – Skipping the creation of a contingency fund forces investors to break long-term investments during emergencies.

IN SHORT

- **Balanced approach to savings and investments** – A healthy financial plan requires striking the right balance between safe savings instruments and growth-oriented investments.
- **Aligning financial planning with life goals** – Investments should not be random; they must be aligned with personal milestones such as education, retirement or buying a home, to ensure long-term financial security.

Risk, Return and Liquidity Comparison of Investments

Investment Type	Risk Level	Expected Return	Liquidity	Example
Savings Account / Fixed Deposit (FD)	Low	Guaranteed, but low	High (easy withdrawal, minor penalty in FD)	Bank Savings, FDs
Government Bonds / SCSS / NSC	Low	Moderate, mostly guaranteed	Moderate (fixed tenure, some premature withdrawal allowed)	SCSS, NSC, Govt Bonds
Mutual Funds (Equity / Hybrid)	Medium to High	Moderate to High (market-linked)	High (redeemable, except ELSS lock-in)	Equity Funds, Balanced Funds
Shares / Equities	High	Potentially high	High (traded on stock exchanges)	NSE/BSE Stocks
Gold / Gold ETFs / SGBs	Medium	Moderate, market-linked	Medium to High (physical gold less liquid)	Gold ETFs, Sovereign Gold Bonds
Real Estate / Property	Medium to High	Moderate to High (depends on market)	Low (selling takes time)	Residential / Commercial Property
APY / UPS / Pension Schemes	Low	Guaranteed pension	Low (fund locked until retirement)	Atal Pension Yojana, UPS

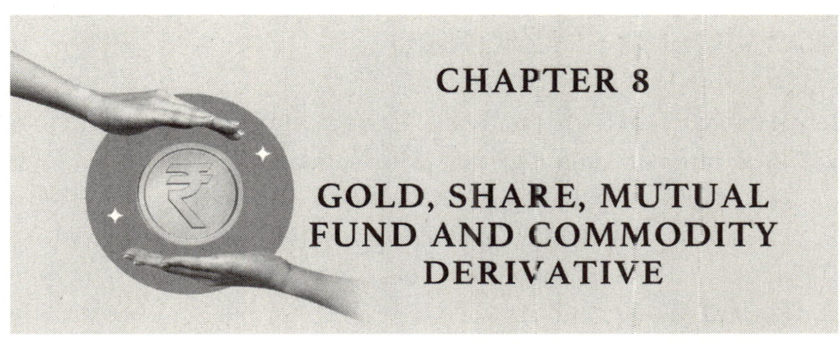

CHAPTER 8

GOLD, SHARE, MUTUAL FUND AND COMMODITY DERIVATIVE

GOLD AS AN INVESTMENT OPPORTUNITY

Gold has long been considered a safe and trusted investment. It acts as a hedge against inflation and economic uncertainty while offering long-term value. Whether in physical form or digital options, gold remains a popular choice for diversifying one's investment portfolio.

WHY INVEST IN GOLD?

Gold has been a trusted asset in India for centuries, valued not just for its cultural importance but also for the financial security it offers. Even today, it remains a preferred investment option for several reasons:

1. Historical Stability – Gold tends to retain its value during economic downturns and is often seen as a safe asset during uncertain times.
2. Portfolio Diversification – Including gold in your investment portfolio helps balance the risk from more volatile assets like shares.
3. Inflation Protection – Unlike paper money, gold maintains its purchasing power, making it a reliable store of value over time.
4. Cultural and Emotional Significance – Gold holds deep traditional value in Indian households, especially during weddings and festivals and is often passed down through generations.
5. Global Liquidity – Gold is easily bought or sold anywhere in the world, providing flexibility and quick access to cash when needed.

WAYS TO INVEST IN GOLD

1. Physical Gold (Jewellery, Coins, Bars)

- **Pros:** It is a tangible asset that offers cultural and traditional value, especially during weddings and festivals.
- **Cons:** Comes with high making charges, risk of theft and additional costs for safe storage such as bank lockers.

2. Digital Gold

- How it works: Platforms like MMTC-PAMP or SAFEGOLD allow buying fractional gold online, stored securely in vaults.
- Pros: No storage hassles, lower entry cost.
- Cons: Dependence on third party to manage your gold may lead to cyber security risk.

MMTC-PAMP stands for Metals and Minerals Trading Corporation of India – PAMP, a joint venture between MMTC Ltd. (a government enterprise) and PAMP SA (a Swiss refiner). It is India's only London Bullion Market Association (LBMA)-accredited gold and silver refinery, producing 24-karat 999.9 purity bullion and digital gold products with international standards of quality and transparency.

PAMP stands for Produits Artistiques Métaux Précieux, which is French for 'Artistic Precious Metals Products'. It is a globally renowned precious metals refinery based in Switzerland. PAMP is known for producing high-quality gold, silver and platinum bars and is accredited by the LBMA. It is trusted worldwide for its purity standards, advanced refining processes and secure storage practices.

SafeGold is a secure digital gold platform that allows users to buy, sell and hold certified 24-carat gold online in small amounts, starting from just a few rupees. The gold is stored in insured vaults under custodial arrangements and owned directly by the user. The platform operates 24/7 via mobile or web and ensures high liquidity and transparency.

3. Gold Mutual Funds

- Invest in gold-related assets such as mining company stocks and gold Exchange-Traded Funds (ETFs).
- **Pros:** Managed by professionals; no need to hold physical gold.

4. Gold Exchange-Traded Funds (ETFs)

- Trade like stocks on exchanges (e.g., Nippon Gold ETF).
- Features:
  - High liquidity (buy/sell anytime)
  - Can be pledged for loans
  - Tracks real-time gold prices

5. Gold Monetization Scheme (GMS)

- Deposit physical gold with banks and earn 2.25–2.50 per cent interest (tax-free)
- Minimum deposit: 10 grams
- Redemption: In cash or gold after maturity
- Tenure: five–seven years (medium term), 10–12 years (long term)
- Lock-in period: three years (medium term), five years (long term)

6. Gold Savings Plans

- Jeweller-led plans: Save small amounts monthly; convert to gold and collect after a fixed period (maturity) with some extra benefits given by the jeweller for the scheme
- Benefits: Disciplined saving, cost averaging (reduces price volatility impact)

7. Sovereign Gold Bonds (SGBs) (Currently Discontinued)

- Last issued in 2024: Existing bonds mature after eight years from issue.
- Features:
  - 2.5 per cent annual interest + gold price appreciation
  - Tax-free redemption
  - Tradable on stock exchanges (if held in Demat)

GOLD FUTURES, OPTIONS AND FORWARDS

Gold futures, options and forwards are all related to speculation on gold for its price fluctuation.

- **Gold Futures:** These are standardized contracts traded on exchanges, obligating the buyer to purchase (or the seller to deliver) gold at a predetermined price on a future date. They are highly liquid and regulated.
- **Gold Options:** These contracts give the holder the right (but not the obligation) to buy (call option) or sell (put option) gold at a particular price (strike price) on or before a specific date. The buyer pays a premium for this flexibility. Unlike futures, options do not require execution if market conditions are unfavourable.
- **Gold Forwards:** These are private, customisable agreements between two parties to buy or sell gold at a particular price on a future date. Unlike futures, forwards are traded OTC and are not standardized, making them less liquid but more flexible in terms of contract terms.

(Note: Physical gold purchases, including considerations like purity and making charges, are discussed separately in Chapter 10.)

Silver as Investment

Historically, like gold, silver is also popular investment. This metal has a cultural value in India.

The different channels of investment in silver are:

1 Purchasing physical silver like coins, bars, ornaments.
2. Silver funds, including ETFs.
3. Digital silver or e-silver platforms, which allow to buyinga fraction of silver.
4 Purchasing silver mining stocks.
5 Invest silver as commodity in commodity exchange.

Gold vs Silver

1. Silver is cheaper and more affordable than gold.
2. Same value of silver needs more storage space than gold.

3. Silver is more volatiles than gold
4. Silver has high demand in industry with respect to gold.
5. Both gold and silver can be used as hedging tools at the time of uncertainty like war, natural calamity, market crash, depression etc.

Over-the-Counter (OTC) refers to financial transactions conducted directly between two parties, rather than through a formal exchange.

It is commonly used for customized contracts such as certain derivatives or private bond deals. While OTC trading offers flexibility, it also involves higher counterparty risk since there is no centralized platform to guarantee the trade.

UNDERSTANDING THE SECURITIES MARKETS

Securities markets are platforms where investors provide funds to businesses and governments by buying financial instruments like shares and bonds. These markets help in the smooth flow of capital, allowing companies to grow and investors to earn returns.

They consist of two key segments:

1. **Primary Market:** This is where new securities such as shares and bonds are issued for the first time to raise capital directly from investors.
2. **Secondary Market:** This is where existing securities are bought and sold among investors, typically through stock exchanges like NSE and BSE.

These markets help allocate savings efficiently, enabling businesses and governments to fund operations while providing investment opportunities.

KEY MARKET TERMINOLOGIES

1. **Money Market:** Deals with short-term, highly liquid instruments

like treasury bills (T-Bills), commercial papers (CPs) and certificates of deposit (CDs). It helps to manage short-term cash needs and influences monetary policy.

National Stock Exchange (NSE) and Bombay Stock Exchange (BSE) are India's two major stock exchanges.

- BSE, established in 1875, is Asia's oldest stock exchange.
- NSE, founded in 1992, is known for its modern electronic trading system and is the largest in India by trading volume.

Both exchanges allow investors to trade in shares, bonds, mutual funds and other financial instruments.

2. **Capital Market:** Focuses on long-term investments, including equities, bonds and derivatives. It supports business expansion and infrastructure projects.
3. **Debt Market:** A platform for trading debt securities like government bonds (G-Secs) and corporate bonds. It provides fixed-income investments with lower volatility compared to equities.

- **Primary Debt Market:** New bonds are issued here.
- **Secondary Debt Market:** Existing bonds are traded based on demand and supply.

SHARES (EQUITIES)

Definition: Shares represent ownership in a company. When you buy shares, you become a part-owner (shareholder) of that company. These are traded on stock exchanges like the NSE and BSE.

Risks: Share prices can fluctuate due to market volatility, company performance, economic conditions and sector trends.

Treasury bills are short term debt instruments issued by the Government of India, currently available for 91 days, 182 days and 364 days. We don't earn interests from treasury bills, the value remains the same, but we can buy them at discounts.	Commercial papers were introduced in India in 1991. These are promissory notes, signed documents that promises a certain amount to be paid on a certain date. Corporates, primary dealers and all-India financial institutions can issue these papers. Corporates can raise short-term resources through commercial papers.	Certificates of deposits are also a type of promissory notes that are issued against money deposited in a bank. Scheduled commercial banks and a few other all-India financial institutions can issue these. Regional rural banks and local area banks cannot issue CDs.

Risk Management: To reduce risk, investors can diversify their investments across different sectors and consider holding shares for the long term to ride out short-term market fluctuations.

- Issuers (companies, governments, banks) raise capital by issuing securities in the market.
- Stock brokers are intermediaries facilitating securities trading on exchanges.
- Asset Management Companies (AMCs) manage pooled investments like mutual funds.

Government Securities (G-Secs) are debt instruments issued by the central or state governments to borrow money from the public. They are considered one of the safest investment options because they are backed by the government. They provide fixed interest and are ideal for conservative investors seeking stable returns with minimal risk.

G-Secs come in various forms, such as

- Treasury Bills (short-term, less than one year)
- Bonds (long-term, ranging from five to forty years)

- Merchant Bankers (Investment Bankers) assist issuers in structuring and launching securities.
- Underwriters guarantee to buy unsold securities in primary markets.
- Initial Public Offering (IPO) is the first time a bond or shares of a company are publicly issued.
- Application Supported by Blocked Amount (ASBA) is an IPO payment method where funds are debited only after the allotment of shares. The amount is blocked at the time of application but is not debited until the shares are allotted.

TYPES OF BONDS

- **Zero-Coupon Bonds:** Issued at a discount and redeemed at face value (no periodic interest).
- **Floating Rate Bonds:** Interest rates adjust periodically based on a benchmark.
- **Callable Bonds:** Issuers can redeem before maturity.
- **Puttable Bonds:** Investors can demand early redemption.

*(**Note:** Discussions on RBI bonds, debentures and corporate bonds are covered in Chapter 8.)*

INVESTING IN SECURITIES: KEY CONSIDERATIONS

Before investing in securities, it is important to assess both market risks and your personal risk tolerance. A thoughtful approach can help minimize potential losses and build long-term wealth. Some key strategies to manage investment risk include:

1. **Asset Allocation:** Spread investments across different asset classes (such as equities, debt and gold) and sectors to balance risk and return.
2. **Systematic Investment Plans (SIPs):** Invest regularly in small amounts to reduce the impact of market volatility and encourage disciplined investing.
3. **Fundamental Analysis:** Study a company's financial health, management quality and business model before making investment decisions.
4. **Avoiding Unverified Tips:** Base your investments on reliable sources and research instead of rumours or unsolicited advice.

PREREQUISITES FOR STOCK MARKET INVESTMENT

To invest in equities, an investor must have the following:

1. **Savings Account:** For fund transfers.
2. **Trading Account:** With a SEBI-registered broker for executing trades.
3. **Demat Account:** For holding securities electronically (via NSDL or CDSL).

Broker and depository details can be verified on SEBI's website (www.sebi.gov.in).

MUTUAL FUNDS

Multiple investors pool their money into a mutual fund and a professional fund manager actively manages it. The fund manager invests this money in a mix of assets such as shares, bonds, money market instruments and other securities based on the fund's objective.

Types of Mutual Funds:

- Equity Funds (High risk, high return)
- Debt Funds (Lower risk, stable returns)

National Securities Depository Limited (NSDL) and Central Depository Services Limited (CDSL) are India's two main depositories that hold your shares in electronic (demat) form. They work like digital lockers for your investments, making trading safer and more convenient by eliminating the need for physical share certificates.

Note: *When you open a demat account, your shares are stored with either NSDL or CDSL, depending on the service provider.*

- Hybrid Funds (Mix of equity and debt)

Exchange-Traded Funds (ETFs)

- Track indices (e.g., Nifty 50), commodities (Gold ETFs) or sectors
- **Pros:** Low expense ratio, real-time trading

INDEX FUNDS

- Passive mutual funds that aim to copy the performance of a specific market index, e.g., Nifty 50 or Sensex.
- **Pros:** Lower fees than active funds.

PRODUCT LABELLING OF MUTUAL FUNDS

As per SEBI guidelines, mutual funds must disclose their risk levels to

Nifty 50 is a stock market index that represents the performance of the top 50 companies listed on the NSE. These companies are selected from

various sectors and reflect the overall health and direction of the Indian stock market. Nifty 50 is often used as a benchmark to measure the performance of mutual funds and other equity investments.

help investors make informed decisions. This standardized labelling ensures transparency, allowing investors to align mutual fund choices with their risk tolerance.

The risk is categorized as follows:

- **Low Risk:** Minimal risk to the principal amount.
- **Low to Moderate Risk:** Slightly higher risk, but principal remains relatively safe.
- **Moderate Risk:** Balanced risk-return profile.
- **Moderately High Risk:** Higher volatility, with potential for greater returns/losses.
- **High Risk:** Significant risk of capital erosion.
- **Very High Risk:** Extreme volatility; principal highly vulnerable to market swings.

SYSTEMATIC INVESTMENT PLAN (SIP)

A SIP enables investors to contribute fixed amounts regularly (monthly, quarterly, etc.) into mutual funds, fostering disciplined savings and long-term wealth creation.

How SIP Works

- Investors commit a predetermined amount (as low as even ₹100) at fixed intervals.
- Investments are automated via post-dated cheques, standing instructions or Electronic Clearing Service (ECS).
- SIP leverages rupee-cost averaging, reducing the impact of market volatility by buying more units when prices are low and fewer when prices rise.

Advantages of SIP

1. Disciplined Investing: Encourages regular savings habits.

2. Avoids Market Timing: Eliminates the need to predict market movements.
3. Rupee-Cost Averaging: Smoothens investment costs over time.
4. Power of Compounding: Small, consistent investments grow significantly over the long term.
5. Affordability: Accessible with minimal initial capital.

Additional SIP Facilities

- Systematic Withdrawal Plan (SWP): Allows periodic withdrawals from investments.
- Systematic Transfer Plan (STP): Facilitates automatic transfers between schemes.

Specialized Investment Fund (SIF): It is a type of investment that bridges the gap between mutual fund (MF) and portfolio management services (PMS).

PMS is a type of professional financial services. With the help of research teams, portfolio managers and stock market experts manage the funds of investors in PMS. PMS is for high-value customers as the minimum investment is ₹50 lakh, whereas minimum investment for SIF is ₹10 lakh. In mutual funds the minimum deposit may even be ₹100.

SIF is regulated by SEBI and managed by SEBI-registered asset management companies.

SIFs offer different types of investment strategies:

1. Equity-Oriented Strategies: Equity long-short funds and sector rotation funds
2. Debt-oriented strategies: debt long-short funds and sectoral debt funds
3. Hybrid strategies: hybrid long-short funds and active asset allocator funds

COMMODITY DERIVATIVES MARKET

The commodity derivatives market is where contracts based on the future prices of natural resources or agricultural products are traded. Instead of trading the actual goods, investors trade in futures and options contracts that derive their value from the price of these commodities. This market helps producers manage price risks and allows investors to profit from price movements. Key categories include:

- Edible Oils and Grains: soybean, wheat, maize
- Bullion: gold, silver
- Metals and Energy: crude oil, copper, natural gas
- Spices and Fibres: turmeric, cotton, jute

Futures and options are financial contracts used to buy or sell assets like shares or commodities at a future date. These are commonly used for speculation or hedging against price changes.

- Futures: A binding agreement to buy or sell at a set price on a specific date.
- Options: Give the right, but not the obligation, to buy or sell at a set price within a certain period.

COMMODITY PRICE RISK

Price fluctuations in commodities can negatively impact both producers (e.g., farmers) and consumers (e.g., manufacturers). Risks include:

- Volatility: Unpredictable price swings.
- Dependence on middlemen: Limited bargaining power for small farmers.
- Storage and financing challenges: Lack of infrastructure and credit access.

HEDGING AGAINST PRICE RISK

Producers and consumers use commodity derivatives (futures, options) to lock in prices, ensuring stability. Hedging is a protection strategy against potential losses caused by price fluctuations. In the commodities market, producers and consumers enter into futures or options contracts to fix the price of a product in advance. It helps to ensure predictable costs and revenues, even if market prices change later.

COMMODITY DERIVATIVE EXCHANGES

Regulated platforms like MCX and NCDEX facilitate trading with:

- Price Discovery: Transparent future pricing.
- Risk Management: Hedging against adverse price movements.

TYPES OF COMMODITY CONTRACTS

1. Forwards: Customized private agreements (OTC)
2. Futures: Standardized exchange-traded contracts (lower default risk)
3. Options:
    - Call Option: Right to buy at a set price
    - Put Option: Right to sell at a set price

Example: A cotton farmer can sell futures to guarantee a fixed price at harvest, shielding against price drops.

Multi Commodity Exchange (MCX) and National Commodity and Derivatives Exchange (NCDEX) are leading commodity exchanges in India. These platforms allow investors, traders and producers to trade commodity derivatives and manage price risks efficiently.

- **MCX** focuses on trading metals, energy products and bullion like gold and crude oil.
- **NCDEX** specializes in agricultural commodities such as wheat, soyabean and spices.

148

BUSINESS AND
FINANCIAL
HEALTH
Mi Operador
14:09

INTRODUCTION

Choosing the proper business structure is a critical decision for any entrepreneur. The type of entity you select impacts legal compliance, liability, taxation and growth potential. India offers various business models, each with distinct features, advantages and regulatory requirements.

DOCUMENTS REQUIRED TO START A BUSINESS IN INDIA

Common documents for business registration include:

- Identity Proof: Aadhaar, PAN, etc.
- Address Proof: Property papers, rent receipts/agreement, utility bill
- Business Registration Forms: Varies with the type of business
- Digital Signature Certificate (DSC): Required for online filings
- Proof of Registered Office: No Objection Certificate (NOC) or rent agreement

ADDITIONAL DOCUMENTS (BASED ON THE TYPE OF BUSINESS):

- Memorandum of Association (MoA): constitution, objectives of the company
- Articles of Association (AoA): Internal governance rules
- LLP Agreement: For Limited Liability Partnerships
- Trust Deed: For NGOs/Section 8 companies

- **MoA** is a legal document required for registering a company in India. It defines the company's scope of operations, its objectives and its relationship with the external world. The MoA lays down the foundation of the company. It includes key details, e.g., the name of the company, registered office address, objectives of the company (main and ancillary), liability of members, capital structure and Association Clause (agreement by initial subscribers). The MoA acts as a company's charter and restricts the company from operating beyond the powers stated in it.

- **AoA** is a legal document that defines the internal rules, regulations and governance structure of a company. While an (MoA) outlines a company's objectives and external scope, the AoA focuses on how it will operate internally. The AoA ensures smooth day-to-day functioning of the company and must not contradict the MoA. It includes details, e.g., rights and duties of directors and shareholders, rules for conducting board and general meetings, procedures for issuing or transferring shares, Dividend distribution policies and Rules for appointing or removing directors.

TYPES OF BUSINESS ENTITIES IN INDIA

1. Sole Proprietorship

- **Ownership:** Single individual
- **Legal Status:** No separate legal identity; owner and business are the same
- **Liability:** Unlimited (personal assets at risk)
- **Compliance:** Minimal regulatory requirements
- **Lifespan:** Ends if the proprietor dies or closes the business
- **Funding:** Difficult to raise capital

Best For: Small businesses, freelancers and local shops

2. One Person Company (OPC)

- **Ownership:** Single promoter (introduced under the Companies Act, 2013)
- **Legal Status:** Separate legal entity
- **Liability:** Limited to business assets
- **Compliance:** Fewer formalities than private companies
- **Conversion:** Must convert to a Private Ltd. Co. if turnover exceeds ₹2 crore

Best For: Sole entrepreneurs seeking limited liability.

3. Partnership Firm

- **Ownership:** 2–20 partners (for banking business, 2-10)
- **Legal Status:** No separate legal identity
- **Liability:** Unlimited (unless LLP)
- **Governance:** Indian Partnership Act, 1932
- **Dissolution:** Ends if a partner exits or dies

Best For: Small businesses with shared ownership (e.g., CA firms, clinics)

4. Limited Liability Partnership (LLP)

- **Ownership:** At least two designated partners
- **Legal Status:** Separate legal entity
- **Liability:** Limited to business assets
- **Compliance:** Mandatory registration under LLP Act, 2008
- **Perpetual Succession:** Continues despite partner changes

Best For: Professionals (lawyers, architects) and SMEs

5. Private Limited Company (Pvt. Ltd)

- **Ownership:** 2–200 shareholders
- **Legal Status:** Separate legal entity
- **Liability:** Limited to shares held
- **Share:** Unlisted, cannot transfer share
- **Compliance:** Strict regulatory filings (MCA, ROC).
- **Fundraising:** Cannot invite public investments.

Best For: Startups and mid-sized businesses.

6. Public Limited Company (PLC)

- **Ownership:** At least seven shareholders (no upper limit)
- **Legal Status**: Separate legal entity
- **Share:** Listed or unlisted; shares traded publicly
- **Liability:** Limited to shareholding
- **Compliance:** Heavy regulatory oversight (SEBI, Companies Act)
- **Capital Raising:** Can issue shares to the public

Best For: Large-scale enterprises seeking public funding

7. Section 8 Company (NGO)

- **Purpose:** Charitable, educational or social welfare
- **Profit Usage:** Reinvested into the organization
- **Legal Status:** Tax-exempt under the Companies Act
- **Ownership:** No dividend distribution to members

Best For: Non-profits, trusts and non-governmental organizations (NGOs)

8. Government Company (PSU)

- **Ownership:** 51 per cent + stake by the central and/or state governments
- **Legal Status:** Registered under the Companies Act
- **Operations:** Subject to government policies
- **Examples:** BHEL, ONGC, SBI

Best For: State-run enterprises in strategic sectors

KEY CONSIDERATIONS WHEN CHOOSING A BUSINESS STRUCTURE

1. **Liability Protection:** Opt for LLP/Company if limiting personal liability is crucial.
2. **Compliance Burden:** Sole proprietorships have fewer regulations than companies.
3. **Funding Needs:** Companies can raise equity; proprietorships rely on personal funds.
4. **Taxation:** Companies face corporate tax; LLPs enjoy pass-through taxation.

5. **Longevity:** Companies have perpetual succession; partnerships dissolve easily.

CLASSIFICATION OF COMPANIES: TYPES AND CHARACTERISTICS

Companies can be categorized based on various factors, including liabilities, listing status, ownership structure, nationality and size. Below is a detailed discussion of these classifications.

1. TYPES OF COMPANIES BASED ON LIABILITIES

a) Company Limited by Shares

In this structure, shareholders' liability is restricted to the unpaid amount on their shares. They are not personally responsible for the company's debts beyond their shareholding. These companies can be further divided into:

- **Private Limited Companies** – Restricted share transfers and fewer shareholders.
- **Public Limited Companies** – Shares can be publicly traded, with more shareholders.

b) Company Limited by Guarantee

Members' liability is limited to a predetermined amount they agree to contribute if the company is wound up. These entities typically lack share capital and are common among non-profit organization, clubs and associations.

c) Unlimited Liability Company

Members bear unlimited responsibility for the company's debts, meaning personal assets can be used to settle obligations.

2. TYPES OF COMPANIES BASED ON LISTING STATUS

a) Listed Companies

Shares are traded on recognized stock exchanges (e.g., BSE, NSE). These

firms must comply with strict SEBI regulations, ensuring transparency and investor protection.

b) Unlisted Companies

Shares are not publicly traded, often held privately by a limited group. While they face fewer regulatory requirements, they must still adhere to the Companies Act, 2013.

3. TYPES OF COMPANIES BASED ON OWNERSHIP STRUCTURE

a) Holding Company

Owns a majority stake in another company (subsidiary), controlling its policies and management without involvement in daily operations.

b) Subsidiary Company

Controlled by a holding company, either fully (Wholly Owned Subsidiary) or partially.

c) Associate Company

A company in which another firm holds a significant (20-50 per cent) but not controlling ownership, allowing it influence without full authority.

4. TYPES OF COMPANIES BASED ON NATIONALITY

a) Indian Company

Incorporated under Indian law, even if the company has shareholders who are from foreign countries or it operates internationally.

b) Foreign Company

Incorporated outside India but conducts business within the country, either directly or through agents.

c) Multinational Company (MNC)

Operates in multiple countries while being headquartered in a single country. For example, Coca-Cola is a foreign multinational company operating in India, while Tata Motors is an Indian multinational company with operations abroad.

5. TYPES OF COMPANIES BASED ON SIZE

The Indian government classifies companies by investments, turnover and employment size:

- **Micro Enterprises** – Investment less than or equal to ₹2.5 crore, annual turnover less than or equal to ₹10 crore.
- **Small Enterprises** – Investment less than or equal to ₹25 crore, annual turnover less than or equal to ₹100 crore.
- **Medium Enterprises** – Investment less than or equal to ₹125 crore, annual turnover less than or equal to ₹500 crore.
- **Large Enterprises** – investment greater than ₹125 crore, annual turnover greater than ₹500 crore i.e., exceeds medium thresholds, often operating nationally or globally with significant economic influence.

These classifications help to determine eligibility for government incentives, subsidies and regulatory benefits, particularly for MSMEs.

MSME UDYAM REGISTRATION: PROCESS AND BENEFITS

Micro, small and medium enterprises (MSME) registration, which is known as Udyam Registration, is an online process that enables businesses to avail various government benefits. While not mandatory, it offers financial and operational advantages, making it highly beneficial for eligible enterprises.

Registration Process

- **Online and Paperless:** The registration is fully digital via the Udyam portal, requiring no document to be uploaded.
- **Self-Declaration Based:** Only an Aadhaar number is needed for proprietors, partners or directors.
- **Automatic Data Fetching:** PAN and GST-linked details (investment, turnover) are pulled from government databases.
- **Integration:** The system connects with Income Tax and GSTIN databases for seamless verification.

Key Benefits of Udyam Registration

1. Lower Interest Rates – Cheaper bank loans compared to regular business loans.
2. Tax Benefits – Extended 15-year carry-forward for Minimum Alternate Tax (MAT) credits.
3. Cost Reductions – Avail a rebate or get some concessions on patents, industry setup and barcode registration.
4. Government Tenders – Priority access via integration with Government eMarketplace (GeM) (a dedicated online market for government organizations or departments as well as public sector undertakings (PSUs) to buy goods and services).
5. Delayed Payment Protection – Legal safeguards against unpaid dues from buyers.
6. Subsidies and Reimbursements – Support for ISO certification, electricity bills and exports.
7. Credit Support – Easier loans under schemes like the Credit Guarantee Scheme and the Credit Linked Capital Subsidy Scheme (CLCSS).
8. Security Deposit Waiver – Reduced costs for participating in e-tenders.
9. Flexibility – Multiple business activities (manufacturing, services or both) under one registration.
10. Global Market Access – Special incentives for participation in international trade fairs.

STARTUP INDIA RECOGNITION AND SEED FUND SCHEME

The Startup India Recognition is a government initiative that provides official recognition to eligible startups, allowing them to access various benefits such as tax exemptions, simplified compliance and support under government schemes. Under this, the Seed Fund Scheme offers financial assistance of up to ₹20 lakh to help early-stage startups with idea validation, product development and market entry. This support enables new ventures to grow without immediate reliance on external investors.

Eligibility for DPIIT Startup Recognition

To qualify as a Startup under the Startup India Initiative, a company must:

- Be less than 10 years old since incorporation.
- Be registered as a Pvt. Ltd. Co., LLP or Partnership Firm.
- Have an annual turnover less than or equal to ₹100 crore since inception.

The **Department for Promotion of Industry and Internal Trade (DPIIT)** is a government body under the **Ministry of Commerce and Industry.** It is responsible for formulating and implementing policies related to industrial growth, foreign direct investment (FDI) and startup development in India.

DPIIT also plays a key role in recognising eligible startups under the **Startup India** initiative, enabling them to avail benefits such as tax exemptions, funding schemes and easier compliance.

- Not formed by splitting an existing business.
- Focus on innovation, scalability and employment generation.

STARTUP INDIA SEED FUND SCHEME (SISFS)

- **Objective:** Provide early-stage funding for proof of concept, prototyping and market entry.
- **Need:** Startups often struggle to secure initial capital before attracting investors or loans.
- **Implementation:**
  - Managed by an Experts Advisory Committee (EAC) under DPIIT.

- Funds are disbursed though incubators supporting eligible startups.
- Supports product trials, commercialization and scaling.

JOINT VENTURES (JV)

A JV is a strategic partnership between two or more entities to collaborate on a specific project.

Key Features:

- Shared Resources: Combines capital, expertise and technology.
- Risk and Reward Sharing: Partners jointly bear costs and profits.
- Flexible Structure: Can be a new entity or a contractual agreement.
- Purpose-Driven: Typically formed for specific projects (e.g., infrastructure, research and development).

COOPERATIVES: DEMOCRATIC BUSINESS MODELS

A cooperative is a business owned and run by its members, who work together to meet shared economic or social needs. Decisions are made democratically, with each member having a say.

Characteristics:

- Equal Voting Rights – One member, one vote (mostly).
- Community-Centric – Focuses on member welfare rather than profit maximization.
- Sector Diversity – Includes agriculture, credit, housing and services.

Examples:

1. Agricultural Credit Societies – Provide loans and financial aid to farmers.
2. Service Cooperatives – Offer marketing, storage and supply chain support.
3. Housing Cooperatives – Manage shared property interests (e.g., apartment societies).

N.B. cooperative housing societies are associations formed by the owners of flats/apartments/property in a locality with common interests and mostly with shared infrastructure. The objective of forming the cooperative housing society is to manage the property of the society better and ensure that interests of all members are protected. Generally each member will have only one voting right, even if the sizes of apartments are different. In a few housing societies, if a member owns more than one apartment, he is given proportional voting rights. It depends on the by-laws; however, the basic principle is that all members are equal.

CHAPTER 10

CONCEPTS OF COST AND FINANCIAL HEALTH

Cost refers to the monetary value of resources used to produce goods or services. It includes materials, labour, expenses and other inputs required for production.

Classification of Costs

A. Element-Based Classification

1. **Materials** – Raw materials (e.g., steel, timber) or components used in production
2. **Labour** – Human effort involved in manufacturing, selling or managing operations
3. **Expenses** – All other costs not classified as materials or labour (e.g., electricity, rent, depreciation)

B. Type-of-Cost-Based Classification

1. **Direct Costs** – Traceable to a specific product (e.g., direct materials, direct labour)
2. **Indirect Costs** – Not directly attributable to a product (e.g., factory maintenance, administrative salaries)

C. Function-Based Classification

1. **Production Costs** – Direct + indirect costs related to manufacturing
2. **Administration Costs** – General management expenses (e.g., office salaries)
3. **Selling and Distribution Costs** – Marketing, logistics and sales-related expenses

4. **R&D Costs** – Expenses for innovation, product development and market research

D. Behaviour-Based Classification

1. **Fixed Costs** – Remain constant regardless of production levels (e.g., rent, management salaries)
2. **Variable Costs** – Change with production volume (e.g., raw materials, direct labour)
3. **Semi-Variable Costs** – Partly fixed and partly variable (e.g., utility bills)

COST SHEET: BREAKUP OF COSTS

A cost sheet is a structured statement summarizing total production costs.

Key Components:

- **Prime Cost** = Direct Materials + Direct Labor + Direct Expenses
- **Works Cost (Factory Cost)** = Prime Cost + Factory Overhead
- **Cost of Production** = Works Cost + Administration Overhead
- **Cost of Sales** = Cost of Production + Selling & Distribution Overhead

Purpose of a Cost Sheet:

- Helps in cost control and comparison with past data.
- Identifies inefficiencies and wastage.
- Useful for pricing decisions and budgeting.

OUTLAY: UNDERSTANDING EXPENDITURE

Outlay refers to the total expenditure incurred to start or operate a business/project.

Types of Outlay:

2. **Capital Outlay** – Long-term investments in assets (e.g., machinery, land).
2. **Operating Outlay** – Day-to-day business expenses (e.g., raw materials, salaries and utilities).

Project Outlay Components:

- **Initial Investments** (e.g., equipment, land).
- **Start-up Costs** (e.g., installation, training).
- **Working Capital** (e.g., raw materials, salaries).

Importance of Outlay Analysis:

- Helps in financial planning and funding decisions.
- Ensures budget adherence and ROI assessment.

Return on Investment (ROI) is a measure used to evaluate how profitable an investment is. It shows the percentage of profit earned compared to the amount of money invested.

Formula: ROI = (Net Profit / Investment Cost) × 100

Example: If you invest ₹10,000 and earn a profit of ₹2,000, your ROI is: (2,000 ÷ 10,000) × 100 = 20 per cent

A higher ROI means a better return on your investment.

STRATEGIC PLANNING & FINANCIAL PERFORMANCE METRICS

Strategic planning is the process of setting long-term goals and deciding how to achieve them. It involves analysing the current situation, identifying opportunities and risks and outlining the steps needed to guide the organization towards growth, competitiveness and sustainability. Financial performance metrics are indicators used to measure a company's financial health and success. Common metrics include net profit margin, ROI, earnings per share (EPS) and debt-to-equity ratio. These help stakeholders assess profitability, efficiency and financial stability.

1. The 3-Year Plan (3YP)

A Three-Year Plan (3YP) is a strategic roadmap outlining a company's objectives, financial projections and growth strategies over a medium-term horizon.

Why a 3YP Works Best

- Balanced Timeframe – Long enough for meaningful growth, yet short enough to adapt to market changes.
- Actionable Goals – Break long-term visions into manageable milestones.
- Avoids Over-Projection – Unlike 5 or 10-year plans, it remains realistic and flexible.

Key Components of a 3YP

1. Company Overview – Mission, vision and current market position.
2. Market Analysis – Industry trends, competition and target audience.
3. Strategic Goals – Revenue targets, expansion plans and innovation strategies.
4. Financial Projections – Expected revenue, expenses and profitability.
5. Execution Plan – Quarterly/yearly actionable steps with key performance indicators (KPIs).

2. TOP LINE VS BOTTOM LINE

Top Line refers to a company's gross revenue or sales. It is the first item on an income statement and reflects how much money a company brings in from its core business operations before any expenses are deducted.

Bottom Line refers to a company's net profit or net income. It appears at the bottom of the income statement and shows the final earnings after subtracting all expenses, taxes and costs.

Top Line (Revenue)

- Refers to gross sales or total revenue before any deductions.

- Indicates sales performance but not profitability.

Ways to Increase Top Line:

- Aggressive marketing and sales expansion
- New product launches
- Price adjustments

Bottom Line (Net Profit)

- Represents net income after all expenses (COGS, taxes, interest, etc.)
- Reflects operational efficiency and cost management

Ways to Improve Bottom Line:

- Cost-cutting (cheaper suppliers, tax benefits)
- Operational efficiency (automation, lean processes)

Key Insight:

- Strong companies grow both top and bottom lines.
- Mature firms may focus on cost optimization if revenue growth stalls.

Purpose of Cost of Goods Sold (COGS): It represents the direct costs involved in producing or purchasing the goods a business sells. It includes materials and labour directly tied to production, but excludes indirect costs like marketing or distribution.

COGS=Opening Inventory+Purchases During the Period–Closing Inventory

3. GROSS PROFIT VS. NET PROFIT

Metric	Calculation	What It Measures
Gross Profit	Revenue – COGS	Profitability before operating expenses
Net Profit	Gross Profit – (Operating Expenses + Taxes + Interest)	Final profit after all costs

Why Both Matter

- Gross Profit → Efficiency in production and pricing
- Net Profit → Overall financial health and sustainability

FINANCIAL STATEMENT ANALYSIS

As an investor, one should read and analyse financial statements which indicate the health and performance of the organization.

A. Income Statement (P&L statement)

- Shows revenue, expenses and profit over a period.
  - Gross Profit = Revenue – Cost of Goods Sold.
  - Net Profit (Bottom Line) = Gross Profit – All other expenses (taxes, interest, etc.).
- Ky Ratios:
  - Profit Margin = (Net Profit / Revenue) x 100 Efficiency in converting sales to profit
  - EPS (Earnings Per Share) = (Net Profit / Outstanding Shares) → Profitability per share
  - P/E Ratio = (Share Price / EPS) → Valuation indicator

B. BALANCE SHEET

A balance sheet is a financial statement that shows a company's financial

position at a specific point in time. It provides a summary of what the company owns (assets), what it owes (liabilities) and the owner's equity.
Formula: Assets = Liabilities + Shareholders' Equity

C. CASH FLOW STATEMENT

A Cash Flow Statement is a financial report that shows the inflow and outflow of cash in a business over a specific period. It helps track how cash is generated and used through different activities, ensuring the company has enough liquidity to meet its obligations. It is divided into three sections, i.e., operating activities, investing activities and financing activities.

- **Tracks cash inflows/outflows from:**
  - Operations (day-to-day business): Cash from core business operations (e.g., receipts from sales, payments to suppliers).
- Healthy sign: Consistent positive cash flow.
  - Investing (asset purchases/sales): Cash used for or received from investments (e.g., purchase or sale of assets).
- Negative number reflects investment in growth, not a loss.
  - Financing (loans, dividends): Cash from or used for financing (e.g., loans, issuing shares, dividend payments).
- High borrowing? Check debt ratios.

CREDIT RATING AND INVESTMENT DECISIONS

Credit Rating (e.g., AAA, BB) reflects an organization's ability to repay its debts on time and indicates the risk of default. It helps investors make informed decisions by evaluating the creditworthiness of companies or financial instruments.

Credit Rating (e.g., AAA, BB) → Assesses timely repayment and default risk.

INFORMED INVESTMENT DECISIONS REQUIRE ANALYSING

Making smart investment choices requires analysing key financial and business indicators to reduce risk and maximize returns. The following areas are essential:

i) Financial statements

These include the balance sheet, income statement and cash flow statement. It provides a detailed view of a company's financial position, performance and cash movements.

ii) Cost structures

Understanding fixed and variable costs helps evaluate how expenses behave with changes in production or sales. This analysis is crucial for assessing profit margins and operational efficiency.

iii) Profitability trends

Reviewing patterns in earnings over time (e.g., rising or falling net profit) reveals whether a business is consistently growing and generating healthy returns.

iv) Market risks

These involve external factors such as economic conditions, competition, inflation or policy changes that could affect the company's performance or share price.

v) Evaluating liquidity and solvency

Liquidity shows the company's ability to meet short-term obligations, while solvency assesses its ability to survive in the long term. Together, they reflect financial health and sustainability.

FINANCIAL RATIOS AND INVESTMENT ANALYSIS GUIDE

Understanding financial ratios is essential for evaluating the performance, stability and profitability of a business. These ratios simplify complex financial data and provide insights that help investors make informed decisions. By analysing aspects such as liquidity, solvency, profitability and efficiency, one can assess a company's financial health and investment potential. This guide introduces key financial ratios and how they are used in practical investment analysis.

1. Key Financial Ratios for Decision Making

Financial ratios help investors, business owners and analysts evaluate a company's performance and make sound financial decisions. These ratios are derived from financial statements and are grouped into key categories:

A. Liquidity Ratios (Short-Term Stability)

Ratio	Formula	Ideal	What It Measures
Current Ratio	Current Assets/ Current Liabilities	2:1	Ability to cover 1-year obligations
Quick Ratio	Quick Assets/ Current Liabilities	1:1	Immediate liquidity without selling inventory

Current assets: Cash and cash equivalents, marketable securities, accounts receivable, inventory, prepaid expenses (such as insurance and rent)

Quick Assets: Cash and cash equivalents, marketable securities, accounts receivable

Insights:

- A current ratio less than one (< 1) signals potential cash flow problems.
- A high quick ratio indicates strong short-term solvency.

B. Solvency/Leverage Ratios (Long-Term Debt Health)

Ratio	Formula	Safe Zone	Risk Indicator
Debt-to-Equity (D/E)	Total Debt / Shareholders' Equity	<1.0	High debt increases bankruptcy risk
Debt Ratio	Total Debt / Total Assets	<100 per cent	>100 per cent means debt exceeds assets

Implications:

- **High D/E** → Heavy reliance on borrowing → Higher interest costs.
- **Low Debt Ratio** → More assets than liabilities → Stronger financial footing.

C. Efficiency Ratios (Asset Utilization)

Ratio	Formula	Interpretation
Asset Turnover	Net Sales / Avg. Total Assets	Higher = Better sales generation from assets
Return on Assets (ROA)	Net Income / Total Assets	Measures profit per rupee of assets
Return on Equity (ROE)	Net Income / Shareholders' Equity	Profitability from shareholder investments

Key Takeaway:

- ROA > ROE suggests efficient debt use.

- Declining Asset Turnover may indicate underused resources.

D. Valuation Ratios (Stock Pricing)

Ratio	Formula	Investor View
Price-to-Book (P/B)	Market Price per Share / Book Value per Share	< 1 = Potentially undervalued
Interest Coverage	Operating Cash Flow / Interest Expense	> 3 = Comfortable debt servicing

Analysis:

- A low P/B stock may be a bargain (but check for hidden risks).
- Weak Interest Coverage → Risk of loan default.

E. Critical Cash Flow Ratios

Ratio	Formula	What It Reveals
Cash Flow to Sales	Operating Cash Flow / Sales	Per cent of revenue turning to cash
Debt Service Coverage	Operating Cash Flow / Total Debt Payments	Ability to repay loans
Dividend Coverage	Operating Cash Flow per Share / Dividends per Share	Sustainability of dividends

Red Flags:

- Negative operating cash flow → Business isn't self-sustaining.

- Dividend Coverage less than (<) 1 → Payouts rely on debt or reserves.

2. CREDIT RATING AGENCIES (CRAS)

Role: Assess default risk of companies/governments.

Top Global Agencies

- Moody's, S&P, Fitch **Indian Agencies (SEBI-Regulated)**
- CRISIL, CARE, ICRA, Brickwork, India Ratings, etc.

Rating Scale

- AAA (Safest) to D (Default)
- **Conflict Risk:** Agencies are paid by issuers → Potential bias.

Investor Tip:

- Compare ratings across agencies.
- A downgrade often triggers stock/bond sell-offs.

4. KEYS TO INVESTMENT SUCCESS

Investment success depends on making informed and disciplined choices. Some of the essential keys include:

Macroeconomic:

- Inflation, interest rates, GDP growth
- Geopolitics (e.g., US-China tensions, wars)

Industry-Specific:

- Supply chain disruptions
- Technological shifts (e.g., AI impact)

Company-Level :

- Quarterly earnings, debt levels
- Management changes

Global Markets:

- US Fed policies, oil prices, currency fluctuations, etc.

CHAPTER 11

QUALITY COUNCIL, ACCREDITATIONS, AUDIT AND COMPLIANCES

The Quality Council of India (QCI) operates as an autonomous body under the Department for Promotion of Industry and Internal Trade (DPIIT), Government of India. It was established in collaboration with leading industry associations, including the Confederation of Indian Industry (CII), the Federation of Indian Chambers of Commerce and Industry (FICCI) and the Associated Chambers of Commerce and Industry (ASSOCHAM). QCI's primary objectives are:

1. Establishing and managing a national accreditation framework to ensure adherence to quality benchmarks.
2. Overseeing the National Quality Campaign, which promotes awareness and adoption of quality standards across industries.

In India, the understanding of quality management remains at a budding stage. There is a pressing need to educate both suppliers and consumers on quality standards, best practices and modern quality control tools. The National Quality Campaign (NQC), funded by the DPIIT, plays a crucial role in this effort. Its initiatives include awareness programmes, industry surveys, publications, media campaigning and specialized training sessions, all conducted by QCI members and professional bodies.

GOVERNANCE AND STRUCTURE OF QCI

The QCI Council, comprising 38 members, represents diverse

stakeholders, including government bodies, industry associations, quality professionals and consumer organizations. A chairperson leads the council, while day-to-day operations are managed by a Secretariat under the Secretary General.

QCI operates through several specialized boards, each focusing on distinct accreditation domains:

- **National Accreditation Board for Certification Bodies (NABCB)** – Accredits certification bodies.
- **National Accreditation Board for Education and Training (NABET)** – Certifies schools and training institutions.
- **National Accreditation Board for Hospitals & Healthcare Providers (NABH)** – Accredits hospitals, clinics and diagnostic centres.
- **National Board for Quality Promotion (NBQP)** – Drives quality awareness initiatives.
- **National Accreditation Board for Testing and Calibration Laboratories (NABL)** – Ensures laboratory competence.

TYPES OF ACCREDITATIONS

1. **Institutional Accreditation** – Evaluates the overall quality of an entire institution.
2. **Programme Accreditation** – Assesses specific academic or professional programmes.
3. **Industry-Specific Accreditation** – Validates compliance with sector-specific standards.
4. **ISO Certification** – Includes ISO 9001 (Quality Management), ISO 14001 (Environmental Management) and other globally recognized standards.
5. **NABET Accreditation** – Ensures quality in education and training providers.
6. **NABCB Accreditation** – Certifies competence in certification bodies.

7. **NABL Accreditation** – Guarantees accuracy in testing and calibration labs.
8. **International Accreditation** – Recognized bodies like **AMBA, AACSB and EQUIS** accredit business schools globally.

The International Organization for Standardization (ISO) is an independent, non-governmental international body that develops and publishes standards to ensure the quality, safety, efficiency and interoperability of products, services and systems across industries worldwide.

Key ISO Standards:

- **ISO 9001** – Quality Management Systems
  Ensures consistent product or service quality, customer satisfaction and continuous improvement in business processes.
- **ISO 14001** – Environmental Management Systems
  Helps organization to manage environmental responsibilities, reduce waste and comply with environmental laws.

Why it Matters:
ISO certification boosts trust, enhances operational efficiency and makes businesses more competitive globally.

AUDIT: EVOLUTION AND IMPORTANCE

The concept of auditing dates back to ancient civilizations, such as Babylonia (2000 BC), where rulers verified financial records to detect fraud. However, modern auditing emerged with the rise of joint-stock companies during the Industrial Revolution (eighteenth century). As businesses expanded, shareholders (owners) delegated management to agents, necessitating independent financial scrutiny to ensure transparency.

Today auditing is a systematic examination of financial records, operational processes and compliance frameworks. It serves multiple purposes:

- Enhancing Credibility – Audited financial statements assure stakeholders of accuracy.
- Error and Fraud Detection – Identifies discrepancies and financial mismanagement.
- Regulatory Compliance – Ensures adherence to legal and industry standards.
- Operational Efficiency – Highlights areas for improvement in business processes.

Different Types of Audits

Businesses implement various types of audits to evaluate their financial health, operational efficiency and regulatory compliance. Each audit serves a distinct purpose, helping organizations identify risks, improve processes and maintain transparency. The key types of audits are discussed below:

1. Internal and External Audit

Internal Audit

- Conducted within the company by its own employees or internal auditors.
- Aims to review financial records, assess risks and evaluate internal controls.
- Helps management and shareholders stay informed about financial performance and alignment with business goals.

- Generally Accepted Accounting Principles (GAAP) is a set of accounting standards used primarily in the United States.
- It ensures consistency and transparency in financial reporting by providing standard rules.
- In India, Indian Accounting Standards (Ind AS) are converged with

International Financial Reporting Standards (IFRS) but still rooted in GAAP principles, which it previously used.
- GAAP is more rules-based, meaning it offers detailed guidelines for financial reporting.

Whereas,
- International Financial Reporting Standards (IFRS) are a globally accepted accounting framework developed by the International Accounting Standards Board (IASB).
- It is followed in more than 140 countries, including the United Kingdom, European Union nations and Australia.
- IFRS is principles-based, offering broader guidelines and requiring more professional judgment.
- India's Indian Accounting Standards (Ind AS) are based on IFRS, helping Indian companies align with global reporting practices.

External Audit
- Performed by independent third-party auditors to ensure objectivity.
- Focuses on verifying the accuracy of financial statements and compliance with accounting standards (e.g., GAAP, IFRS).
- Enhances credibility for investors, regulators and stakeholders by providing an unbiased financial assessment.

Key Difference:
- Internal audits focus on process improvement and risk management.
- External audits ensure financial transparency and legal compliance.

2. COST AUDIT
- Evaluates the accuracy of cost accounting records and adherence to cost management policies.
- Ensures efficient resource allocation and identifies cost-saving opportunities.

- **Involves:**
  - Verification of cost reports, statements and accounting techniques.
  - Assessment of compliance with cost accounting principles and regulatory requirements.

Significance: Helps businesses optimize expenses and improve financial decision-making.

3. PERFORMANCE AUDIT

- Assesses operational efficiency, effectiveness of programmes and achievement of business objectives.
- **Evaluates:**
  - Internal controls and risk management.
  - Productivity of business processes.
  - Outcomes of organizational strategies.

Use Case: Commonly used in government agencies, NGOs and large corporations to measure programme success.

4. COMPLIANCE AUDIT

- Examines whether a business follows legal, regulatory and internal policies.
- Common in highly regulated industries (e.g., healthcare, finance, education).
- Ensures adherence to:
  - Government laws (e.g., labour, environmental regulations).
  - Industry standards (e.g., ISO).

Outcome: Reduces legal penalties and enhances corporate governance.

5. OPERATIONAL AUDIT

- Analyses business processes, policies and workflows to identify inefficiencies.

- Can be conducted internally or by external consultants.
- **Focuses on:**
  - Process optimization
  - Resource utilization
  - Goal alignment with organizational strategies

Benefit: Improves overall business performance and cost-effectiveness.

6. MANAGEMENT AUDIT

- Evaluates the effectiveness of leadership in implementing business strategies.
- **Assesses:**
  - Decision-making processes
  - Resource management
  - Regulatory and policy compliance

Purpose: Ensures strong corporate governance and strategic alignment.

7. STATUTORY AUDIT

- Mandated by law (e.g., Companies Act, 2013).
- Conducted by external auditors to verify financial statements.
- **Ensures:**
  - Accuracy of financial reports
  - Compliance with corporate laws

Impact: Builds trust among investors and regulators.

8. TAX AUDIT

- Legally required for businesses exceeding a specified income/turnover threshold.
- Examines accounting records for tax compliance (under Income Tax Act, 1961).
- Prevents tax evasion and ensures accurate tax filings.

Applicability: Mandatory for companies, LLPs and high-income professionals.

9. PAYROLL AUDIT

- Reviews payroll records to detect errors, fraud or compliance gaps.
- Conducted internally or by external auditors.
- **Ensures:**
  - Correct salary calculations.
  - Proper tax deductions.
  - Adherence to labour laws.

Benefit: Prevents legal disputes and financial discrepancies.

A payroll audit is a detailed review of an organization's payroll processes to ensure accuracy, compliance and consistency. It involves checking employee records, salary payments, tax deductions and statutory contributions (such as Provident Fund, Employee State Insurance and TDS) against applicable labour laws and internal policies.

The purpose of a payroll audit is to:

- Identify errors or discrepancies in salaries, bonuses or deductions
- Ensure timely tax payments and filings
- Verify proper classification of employees (full-time, contract, etc.)
- Detect possible fraud or non-compliance

Regular payroll audits help maintain financial integrity and avoid penalties from regulatory authorities.

10. INFORMATION SYSTEM (IT) AUDIT

- Assesses IT infrastructure, cybersecurity and data integrity.
- **Common in tech-driven firms to:**
  - Identify IT risks.
  - Prevent cyber threats.
  - Ensure compliance with data protection laws

Outcome: Enhances data security and system reliability.

➢ **Green Data Centres and Sustainable IT Are Rising**
Cloud infrastructure is evolving towards sustainability with green data centres, featuring renewable energy, efficient cooling and modular design. These practices help reduce environmental impact while powering AI and digital ecosystems.

➢ **Self-Healing Software Revolutionizes IT Resilience**
Emerging technologies now monitor systems in real time, detect anomalies and automatically repair issues. It ensures continuous performance and strengthens cybersecurity without human intervention.

II. FORENSIC AUDIT

- Investigates financial fraud, embezzlement or legal disputes.
- Conducted by forensic accountants for legal evidence.
- **Used in cases of:**
  - Suspected fraud
  - Corporate litigation
  - Regulatory investigations

Significance: Supports legal proceedings and fraud recovery.

REGULATORY COMPLIANCE IN INDIA: A COMPREHENSIVE GUIDE FOR BUSINESSES

Compliance with legal and regulatory requirements is fundamental for any business operating in India. Proper adherence not only prevents penalties but also strengthens stakeholder confidence and enhances corporate reputation. This guide outlines key compliance obligations, from incorporation of the company to annual filings and sector-specific regulations, to ensure businesses operate within the legal framework.

1. Incorporation and Business Commencement

Establishing a business in India requires meticulous documentation and approvals. Key steps include:

i) Incorporation Documentation

- **Company Identification Number (CIN):** Mandatory for legal recognition.
- **Director Identification Number (DIN):** Required for all directors.
- **Memorandum of Association (MOA) & Articles of Association (AOA):** Define the company's objectives, structure and governance rules.

ii) Commencement of Business

- Companies must file a Commencement of Business Certificate within 180 days of incorporation.
- Failure to comply may lead to striking off the company's name from the Registrar of Companies (RoC).

2. Annual Compliance Requirements

After incorporation, companies must fulfil ongoing obligations:

i) Board Meetings

- Minimum four meetings per year (at least one every quarter).
- Quorum requirements and proper minutes documentation are mandatory.

ii) Annual General Meeting (AGM)

- Must be conducted within six months of the financial year-end.
- Notices, resolutions and minutes must be filed with the RoC.

iii) Financial Statements & Annual Returns

- Audited financial statements must be filed with the Ministry of Corporate Affairs (MCA).
- Annual Return (Form MGT-7) submission is compulsory.

iv) KYC Compliance

- Directors and promoters must submit KYC details (DIR-3 KYC) annually.

v) Disclosure of Significant Transactions

- Related-party transactions exceeding prescribed thresholds must be disclosed.

➢ **Form MGT-7: Annual Return of a Company** is a statutory return that companies registered in India must file annually with the Ministry of Corporate Affairs (MCA) under the Companies *Act, 2013.*

Purpose: It contains key details of the company's

- registered office and principal business activities
- shareholding pattern
- details of directors, key managerial personnel and meetings
- financial summary and indebtedness
- changes in ownership, if any.

Applicability: All companies, except One Person Companies (OPCs), must file Form MGT-7. It must be certified by a Company Secretary (in practice), if applicable.

Due Date: Within 60 days from the date of the AGM.

➢ **Form DIR-3 KYC: Director KYC Compliance** is a mandatory form that every individual who has been allotted a **DIN** must file annually with the MCA.

Applicability: All directors with a valid DIN as on 31 March of the financial year must file DIR-3 KYC by the specified due date.

Due Date and Penalty:

- Due date: Usually 30 September each year
- Penalty: ₹5,000 if filed after the due date; DIN gets deactivated until compliance is restored.

3. Audit Compliance

Audits ensure financial transparency and regulatory adherence:

i) Statutory Audits

- Mandatory for all companies under the Companies Act, 2013.
- Conducted by a certified statutory auditor.

ii) Audit Reports

- Auditors must submit reports to the MCA and shareholders.

iii) Internal Controls

- Companies must implement fraud-proof financial systems.

iv) Audit Committee

- Listed companies and large corporations must form an independent audit committee.

4. Compliance Based on Company Size & Type

Requirements vary depending on business structure and revenue:

i) Independent Directors

- Listed companies must appoint at least one-third independent directors.

ii) Corporate Social Responsibility (CSR)

- **Companies with:**
  - ₹500 crore+ net worth
  - ₹1,000 crore+ turnover
  - ₹5 crore+ net profit

  must spend 2 per cent of average net profit on CSR activities.

iii) Secretarial Compliance

- Listed companies must appoint a Company Secretary (CS).
- In case of paid-up capital of ₹10 crore or more for other public and private companies.

iv) Share Capital Regulations

- Compliance with issuance, buyback and redemption rules is mandatory.

v) Licenses & Registrations

- Sector-specific permits (e.g., FSSAI for food businesses, GST for taxation).
- The effect of non-compliance may be a penalty or disruption of operation.

Corporate Social Responsibility (CSR) refers to a company's voluntary and statutory commitment to contribute to the social, environmental and economic well-being of society. It goes beyond profit-making to include ethical practices, sustainable development and community engagement.

In India, CSR became mandatory under Section 135 of the Companies Act, 2013. Companies meeting certain financial thresholds are required to spend at least 2% of their average net profits (of the last three financial years) on CSR activities.

Latest Developments in CSR:

1. **Enforcement of CSR Obligations**: Over the past three years, the Indian government has penalized 30 companies for failing to comply with CSR spending requirements under the Companies Act, 2013
2. **CSR Spending Set to Multiply**: CSR expenditure in India is projected to more than three times from ₹35,000 crore in 2023–24 to over ₹1.2 lakh crore by 2034–35. However, distribution remains uneven, with only 2–4% of funds reaching marginalized regions. Experts call for more inclusive and experimental approaches to CSR.
3. **Transformative Projects, Real Impact Examples:**

- In Gujarat, CSR funding has upgraded mortuary infrastructure across cities like Vadodara and Surat improving storage and postmortem capacity in response to emergencies.
- In Bengaluru, a dried-up lake was revived into a fresh, usable water body through a CSR initiative, benefiting both the environment and the local community.

ESG

In 2025, a parliamentary panel urged amendments to the Companies Act, 2013 to embed Environmental, Social and Governance (ESG) considerations within directors' fiduciary duties and establish a dedicated oversight body for enforcing ESG norms.

5. Other Key Compliances

i) Statutory Registers Maintenance

- The register of Members, Directors and Charges must be updated regularly.

ii) Internal Controls & Risk Management

- Fraud detection systems and financial safeguards are critical.

iii) Disclosure & Investor Relations

- SEBI regulations require timely disclosures for listed companies.

iv) Tax Compliance

GST, TDS and Income Tax Return filings must be submitted on time to avoid penalties.

Navigating India's regulatory landscape requires a structured compliance strategy from incorporation documentation to annual audits and sector-specific filings. Proactive adherence not only minimizes legal risks but also enhances credibility with investors, regulators and customers. Businesses must stay updated with evolving laws to ensure long-term sustainability and growth.

BORROWING AND DEBT MANAGEMENT

CHAPTER 12

UNDERSTANDING DIFFERENT TYPES OF LOANS

Loans are important financial tools that help individuals and organizations meet their funding needs when immediate resources are not available. They differ, based on purpose, collaterals, eligibility and repayment terms, making it essential for borrowers to choose the right type of loan according to their specific requirements. Such as:

PERSONAL LOAN

A personal loan is an unsecured loan offered by banks and financial institutions to meet diverse financial needs such as medical emergencies, education expenses, debt consolidation, home renovation or travel. Since no collateral is required, approval is based on the borrower's creditworthiness, income and repayment capacity.

Key Features and Benefits

- **Unsecured:** No collateral needed
- **Flexible Usage:** Can be used for multiple purposes
- **Quick Disbursal:** Many lenders approve and disburse within hours
- **Tenure Options:** Typically, one–five years
- **Loan Amount:** Usually ranges from ₹10,000 to ₹50 lakh, depending on income and credit score

Factors Affecting Eligibility

- **Credit Score (CIBIL ≥ 750 preferred)** – A low score may lead to rejection or higher interest rates.
- **Monthly Income** – Determines repayment capacity.

- **Work Experience** – Minimum 1 or 2 years (varies from bank to bank) of stable employment.
- **Existing Liabilities** – A high debt-to-income ratio reduces approval chances.
- **Age Limit** – Roughly 21–60 years and some lenders even allow up to 80 years.

The Credit Information Bureau (India) Limited (CIBIL) is India's leading credit information company. It maintains credit records of individuals and businesses, including loans and credit cards, as reported by member banks and financial institutions. A CIBIL Score (ranging from 300 to 900) reflects a person's creditworthiness. Higher scores increase the chances of loan approval and access to better interest rates

Documents Required

- ID and Address Proof (Aadhaar, PAN, Passport)
- Salary slips (last 3 months)
- Bank statements (last 6 months)
- Income Tax Returns (ITR)

Things to Consider Before Applying

- **Interest Rates:** Usually at 10-36 per cent per annum and are subject to change from time to time. Compare different lenders to find the best deal.
- **Prepayment Penalties:** Some banks charge an additional fee for early loan closure.
- **Processing Fees:** Typically 1–3 per cent of the loan amount.

Application Process

1. Check eligibility (income, credit score).
2. Compare lenders (banks vs. NBFCs).
3. Submit documents online/offline.
4. Await approval and disbursal (24 hrs to 7 days).

HOME LOAN

A home loan is a secured loan provided by a bank or financial institution to help individuals purchase, construct or renovate a residential property. The property itself serves as collateral until the loan is fully repaid. Home loans usually have longer repayment periods and offer competitive interest rates, making them a common choice for financing real estate.

Types of Home Loans

- Purchase Loan – For buying a new house/flat
- Plot Loan – For purchasing land
- Construction Loan – For building a house on owned land
- Composite loan – both land and house construction
- Home Improvement Loan – For repairs/renovations
- Balance Transfer Loan – To shift an existing loan to a lower-interest lender
- Top up: Extra fund borrowing from the existing home loan

Eligibility Criteria for Home Loans

- **Credit Score:** 750+ preferred (CIBIL/Experian)
- **Age:** 23–70 years (varies by lender)
- **Income:** Minimum ₹25,000/month (salaried); ₹3L/year (self-employed)
- **Employment Stability:** 2+ years in current job/business
- **Property Valuation:** The bank assesses the market value before approval

Documents Required

- **Identity Proof:** Aadhaar, PAN, Passport
- **Address Proof:** Utility bills, Rental agreement
- **Income Proof:**
    - **Salaried:** 3 months' payslips + Form 16
    - **Self-employed:** 2 years ITR + Profit/Loss statements
- **Property Papers:** Sale deed, NOC, Approved plan

Home Loan Application Process

1. Check eligibility (online calculators or bank visit).
2. Compare lenders (interest rates, processing fees).
3. Submit documents (online/offline).
4. Property verification (bank inspection).
5. Loan sanction and disbursal (7–15 days).

Home Loan Interest Rates

- Average range: 7–9 per cent p.a., subject to change from time to time

Factors affecting rates:

- RBI repo rate fluctuations
- Inflation and economic conditions
- Borrower's credit profile

Fixed vs. Floating Interest Rates

Fixed Rate	Floating Rate
Remains constant for a fixed period (e.g., 3–5 years)	Changes with market conditions (RBI repo rate)
Predictable EMIs (no sudden hikes)	EMIs may increase/decrease based on rate revisions
Higher initial rate than floating	Lower initial rate, but risky if rates rise sharply

Possible special concessions for:

- Women borrowers
- Employees of lending bank
- Senior citizens (even short-duration loans)

Tax Benefits of Home Loans:

- ₹1.5 lakh deduction on principal repayment under Section 80C.
- ₹2 lakh deduction on interest payment under Section 24B.
- Interest Rates: Generally, 7–9 per cent p.a., which is lower than most personal loans.
- Long Tenure: Repayment periods can be up to 30 years, helping reduce the EMI burden.
- No Prepayment Penalty: Applicable for floating rate loans. Fixed-rate loans may attract a prepayment penalty.

EDUCATION LOAN – FINANCING YOUR ACADEMIC DREAMS

With rising education costs in India and abroad, many students rely on education loans to fund their studies. These loans cover tuition, living expenses and other academic fees, ensuring financial constraints do not hinder education.

Types of Education Loans

- **Undergraduate Loans** – For bachelor's degrees after 12th grade
- **Postgraduate Loans** – For master's or doctoral programmes
- **Career-Oriented Loans** – For vocational training, diplomas and skill development courses
- **Parent-Sponsored Loans** – Parents can take out loans for their children's education

Key Features of Education Loans

- **Loan Amount** – Up to ₹1.5 crore, depending on the course and institution.
- **Repayment Tenure** – Flexible repayment options, extending up to 15 years.
- **Moratorium Period** – EMI repayment begins 6–12 months after course completion or employment, whichever is earlier
- **Interest Rates** – Range of 4 to 16 per cent (varies with lender).
- **Tax Benefits** – Under Section 80E of the Income Tax Act, borrowers can claim deductions on interest paid.

Eligibility Criteria

- Admission to a recognized university/institution (in India or abroad).
- For undergraduate courses: Completion of 10+2.
- For postgraduate courses: A prior degree is mandatory.

Required Documents

- Admission letter from the institution
- Academic records (marksheets, certificates)
- Identity and address proof (Aadhaar, PAN, passport)
- Income proof (salary slips, ITR, bank statements)
- Collateral documents (if applicable)

Expenses Covered Under Education Loans

- Tuition and examination fees
- Hostel and accommodation charges
- Travel expenses (for international students)
- Cost of books, laptops and study materials
- Insurance premiums and caution deposits
- Research and project-related expenses

Additional Benefits

- **Preferential Interest Rates** – Some banks offer lower rates for female students or children of bank employees.
- **Pre-Visa Disbursement** – Certain lenders disburse loans before visa approval for abroad studies.
- **Doorstep Documentation** – Many banks provide document collection services for convenience.

CAR LOAN

A car loan is a secured loan provided by a bank or financial institution to help individuals purchase a new or used car. The vehicle itself serves as collateral until the loan is repaid in full. Car loans typically come with fixed or variable interest rates, flexible repayment tenures and may require a down payment depending on the lender's terms.

Features and Benefits

Loan Amount: Up to 90 per cent of a car's on-road price (some lenders offer 100 per cent financing).

Interest Rates: 7–10 per cent p.a. (varies by lender and credit score).

Tenure: 1–7 years (longer tenure = lower EMI but higher interest).

Secured Loan: the car acts as collateral until repayment.

Quick Processing: 24-hour approval (pre-approved offers).

Eligibility and Documents

- Eligibility:
  - **Age:** 21–65 years
  - **Income:** ₹20,000+ (salaried); ₹3 lakh/year (self-employed)
  - **Employment:** 1+ year in current job/business
- Documents:
  - **ID and Address Proof (Aadhaar, PAN, Voter ID)**
  - Income Proof (Salary slips/ITR for 2 years)
  - Car Quotation (from dealer)
  - Driving Licence (compulsory for loan disbursal)
  - Utility Bill (telephone/electricity bill as address proof for the company)
  - Bank statement

Factors Affecting Car Loan Approval

- **Credit Score (650+ ideal)** – Lower score = higher interest/rejection
- **Debt-to-Income Ratio (DTI < 40 per cent)** – High existing loans reduce eligibility
- **Down Payment (10–20 per cent recommended)** – Lower borrowing = less interest
- **Car Age (for used cars):**
  - **Up to five years old** – Easier approval
  - **Older cars** – Higher interest or rejection

What to do before taking a Car Loan

1 Research on lenders (compare interest rate).

2 Research on dealers (compare prices and offers).

3 Check eligibility and necessary documents.

4 Calculate EMI (if the tenure is less, then the EMI is more).

5. Apply with the necessary documents.

Key Tips Before Applying

- Compare Interest Rates (Even a 0.5 per cent difference = big savings).
- Negotiate Processing Fees (0.5–2 per cent of loan amount).
- Avoid Long Tenures (Higher total interest cost).
- Watch for Hidden Charges (Prepayment penalty, insurance bundling).
- Check Festival Discounts (Diwali, New Year offers).

Comparison: Home Loan vs. Car Loan

Parameter	Home Loan	Car Loan
Loan Amount	Up to 90 per cent of property value	Up to 90-100 per cent of car price
Tenure	Up to 30 years	Up to 7 years
Interest Rate	7–9 per cent	7–10 per cent
Tax Benefits	Yes (under Sec 24 and 80C)	No
Collateral	Property Mortgaged	Car hypothecated

BUSINESS LOANS – FUELLING GROWTH AND EXPANSION

Business loans provide capital for startups, MSMEs and established businesses.

Types of Business Loans

1. **Term Loans** – For long-term investments (machinery, expansion)
2. **Working Capital Loans** – For daily operational expenses
3. **Startup Loans** – For new entrepreneurs

Eligibility and Documents

- Sole Proprietors, Firms and Companies are eligible.
- **Documents:**
  - KYC (PAN, Aadhaar).
  - Business registration proof.
  - Bank statements and ITR

Government Schemes

- Pradhan Mantri MUDRA Yojana (PMMY)
  - Loans up to ₹20 lakh for MSMEs.
- Categories:
  - Shishu (up to₹50,000),
  - Kishor (above ₹50,000 - up to ₹5 lakh),
  - Tarun (above ₹5 lakh – up to ₹10 lakh),
  - Tarun Plus (above ₹10 lakh – up to ₹20 Lakh).

Startup India Seed Fund Scheme

- Grants up to ₹50 lakh for prototypes and market entry.
- DPIIT creates it.
- An Expert Advisory Committee monitors it

Eligibility: less than two years after incorporation

- PSB Loans in 59 Minutes
  - Instant approval (within 59 minutes, i.e., less than one hour) for MSME loans (up to ₹5 crore).
  - Processed digitally with advanced technology
  - Interest rate starts from around 8.5 per cent per annum and may vary over time depending on factors such as credit score, loan amount and lender policies.
  - Lenders: Both public and private sector banks and NBFCs
  - Duration: short term to 15 years

Udyogini Scheme

- For women entrepreneurs (age 18–55 years)
- Small business: trader, retailer, producer
- Loan up to ₹3 lakhs
- Interest rate: Generally, 6 per cent, may be free (for disabled people, Dalits and widows)

AGRICULTURE LOANS – FINANCING FARMERS' NEEDS

Agriculture loans ensure liquidity for farmers for various farming activities, including cultivation, livestock-rearing, horticulture and purchasing equipment. These loans help farmers manage expenses for inputs like seeds, fertilizers, labour and machinery.

Types of Agriculture Loans

1. Crop Loan (Kisan Credit Card (KCC))
   - Short-term loan for seasonal farming needs.
   - Farmers receive a Kisan Credit Card for easy withdrawals.
2. Agricultural Term Loan
   - Long-term financing for equipment, irrigation and infrastructure.
   - Repayment tenure up to four years.
3. Solar Pump Set Loan
   - Funds for solar-powered irrigation systems.
   - Tenure up to 10 years.
4. Loan for Allied Activities
   - Supports dairy farming, fisheries, poultry, etc.
5. Farm Mechanization Loan
   - For purchasing tractors, harvesters and other machinery.
6. Agricultural Gold Loan
   - Gold-backed loan for urgent farming needs.
7. Forestry and Horticulture Loans
   - For tree-based farming, orchards and land development.

Key Features of Agriculture Loans

- Interest Rates: Starting around 9 per cent p.a.
- Processing Fees: 0–4 per cent of the loan amount.
- Loan Types: Crop loans, term loans, gold loans and specialized loans for allied activities.
- Repayment Tenure: From short-term (seasonal) to long-term (up to 10 years).

Eligibility Criteria

- Age: 18–70 years.
- Must own agricultural land or assets for collateral.
- Can apply individually or jointly.

Documents Required

- KYC documents (Aadhaar, PAN, Voter ID)
- Land ownership papers
- Bank statements (if applicable)

How to Apply?

- Visit a bank/NBFC branch or apply online.
- Submit documents and await approval (fast processing).

GOLD LOANS – A QUICK AND SECURE FINANCING SOLUTION

A gold loan is a type of secured loan where borrowers pledge their gold ornaments or jewellery as collateral to obtain immediate funds. Since the loan is backed by physical gold, lenders offer competitive interest rates and quick disbursal, making it an ideal option for financial emergencies.

Key Features of Gold Loans

1. Loan Amount and Valuation:

- The loan amount depends on the current market value of the gold pledged.
- Most lenders offer 75–90 per cent of the gold's value, with maximum limits varying by institution (some go up to ₹1.5 crore).

- Gold purity must be 18 carats or above for eligibility.

2. Interest Rates and Charges

- Interest rates typically range between 7 and 29 per cent p.a., depending on the lender and loan tenure.
- **Additional charges may include:**
  - **Processing fees** (0.5 – 2 per cent of the loan amount)
  - **Valuation fees** (for assessing gold purity)
  - **Late payment penalties** (if EMIs are delayed)

3. Flexible Repayment Options

Borrowers can choose from multiple repayment methods:

- EMI-based repayment (monthly instalments)
- Interest-only payments (pay interest monthly, principal at the end)
- Bullet repayment (pay full principal + interest at maturity)

4. Loan Tenure

- Generally short-term (three months) to medium-term (up to four years).
- Some lenders allow tenure extensions with revised terms.
- Some lenders provide even a seven-day tenure

5. Quick Disbursal and Minimal Documentation

- Gold loans are processed faster than unsecured loans (often within hours).
- Minimal paperwork is required compared to personal or business loans.

Eligibility Criteria for Gold Loans

- Age: Minimum 18 years (some lenders require 21+).
- Gold Ownership: Must legally own the gold being pledged.
- No Income Proof Needed: Unlike other loans, gold loans do not require salary slips or income verification.

Documents Required

- Identity Proof (Aadhaar, PAN, Voter ID and Passport)
- Address Proof (Utility bills, Aadhaar and Rental Agreement)

- Passport-sized photographs
- Gold Purity Certificate (if available)

How to Apply for a Gold Loan?

1. Online Application

- Visit the lender's website and select the gold loan option.
- Fill in personal details, gold weight and purity.
- Submit documents digitally (if applicable).
- Get approval and visit the branch for gold valuation and disbursal.

2. Offline (Branch) Application

- Locate the nearest bank/NBFC branch.
- Carry gold jewellery for valuation and deposit.
- Submit KYC documents and complete the application.
- Receive funds on the same day after verification.

Important Factors to Consider Before Taking a Gold Loan

1. Loan-to-Value (LTV) Ratio

- RBI mandates a maximum 75 per cent LTV for gold loans, meaning you can borrow up to 75 per cent of the gold's market value.
- Some NBFCs may offer higher LTV (up to 90 per cent) but at higher interest rates.

2. Interest Rate Comparison

- Compare rates across banks, NBFCs and fintech lenders for the best deal.
- Some lenders offer discounts (1-2 per cent) for timely interest payments.

3. Hidden Charges

- Check for processing fees, prepayment penalties and late fees.
- Opt for lenders with no foreclosure charges if you plan early repayment.

4. Safety of Gold

- Ensure the lender has secure vaults and insurance for pledged gold.

- Verify the return policy; some lenders deduct storage fees if gold is not reclaimed on time.

5. Repayment Flexibility

- Choose a repayment plan that aligns with your cash flow (EMIs, bullet payments or interest-only).
- Avoid defaulting, as lenders can auction the gold to recover dues.

7. CONSUMER DURABLE LOANS – BUY NOW, PAY LATER

A consumer durable loan helps one to purchase electronics and appliances like TVs, laptops and washing machines, etc, on EMI.

Key Features

- Loan Amount: ₹10,000 to ₹15 lakh
- Interest Rate: Often marketed as '0 per cent EMI' (but check hidden costs)
- Tenure: Up to 36 months
- No Collateral Needed (mostly unsecured)

Eligibility and Documents

- Salaried/Self-Employed individuals are eligible.
- **Documents:**
  - ID/Address Proof (Aadhaar, PAN)
  - Income Proof (Salary slips/ITR for self-employed)

Benefits

- No-cost EMI options
- Quick approval (same-day disbursal)
- No foreclosure charges

EMI and Repayment

- **Equated Monthly Instalment (EMI)** = Principal + Interest (spread over loan tenure).
- **Loan Tenure:**
  - Personal Loans: 1–7 years
  - Business Loans: Up to 10 years (longer for secured loans)

- Housing Loans: Generally long term, such as 5/20/25 years

Step-by-step loan application

- Select a lender after conducting thorough research and gathering proper information.
- Visit the branch office of the bank/finance company and also visit their official website.
- Then submit a loan application with the necessary documents to the branch office or upload those online.
- The lender will process the loan application and sanction.

CONSEQUENCES OF LOAN DEFAULT

Defaulting on loans leads to severe repercussions:

Impact	Description
Credit Score Damage	Drops significantly (hard to get future loans)
Legal Action	Lender can file a lawsuit
Asset Seizure	For secured loans (home, car, gold)
Debt Recovery Agents	Harassment calls and visits
Bankruptcy Risk	In extreme cases

Solution: If struggling, negotiate restructuring or settlement with the lender.

UNDERSTANDING BORROWER RIGHTS AND LENDER PROTECTIONS IN LOAN AGREEMENTS

Taking a loan comes with the responsibility of making timely repayments, but unforeseen financial difficulties can sometimes disrupt this process. Missing payments may lead to default and expose borrowers to potential harassment. However, borrowers have legal protections to ensure fair treatment during debt recovery. Financial institutions must follow strict guidelines when dealing with defaulters to safeguard the rights of all parties involved, including borrowers, lenders and collection agencies.

Many lenders outsource debt collection to specialized agencies, as this can be more cost-effective than maintaining in-house teams. These agencies, often called recovery agents, usually work on commission, which incentivizes them to collect dues. However, they must operate within legal boundaries and avoid unethical practices.

The RBI strictly prohibits harassment, which includes public shaming, privacy violations, intimidation or undue pressure. Despite regulatory safeguards, weak enforcement and lack of borrower awareness sometimes led to unethical recovery tactics. Even in default, borrowers retain their rights. The RBI ensures that lenders treat borrowers with dignity and respect.

Below are key borrower protections:

1. **Right to Receive a Notice:** Before taking severe actions like asset seizure, lenders must issue a formal notice. This provides borrowers with an opportunity to settle dues or negotiate repayment terms. If unresolved, the account may be classified as a non-performing asset (NPA), leading to further recovery measures, including asset liquidation.
2. **Right to Receive Surplus from Asset Sale:** If a borrower's assets are sold to recover debt and the sale proceeds exceed the owed amount, the borrower is entitled to get the surplus amount after deducting applicable fees.
3. **Right to Fair Debt Collection Practices:** The RBI's Fair Practices Code (FPC) mandates ethical debt recovery. Borrowers must not face abuse, threats or harassment from recovery agents.
4. **Right to Grievance Redressal:** If borrowers experience unfair

treatment, they can escalate complaints through the lender's grievance mechanism or approach the Banking Ombudsman for unresolved disputes.

5. **Right to Legal Assistance:** Borrowers can seek legal counsel if facing disputes over loan terms or recovery methods. Legal experts can guide them through dispute resolution options.
6. **Right to Accurate Credit Reporting:**
   Credit Information Companies (CICs) maintain credit reports under RBI supervision. Borrowers can access their reports and, in case of inaccuracies, resolve them through formal channels.

In India, a loan is classified as a non-performing asset (NPA) if the borrower fails to make interest or principal payments for ninety days or more. After the 2008 global financial crisis, NPAs became a major concern for Indian banks, with gross NPAs peaking at over ₹10 lakh crore in 2018, prompting large-scale reforms like the Insolvency and Bankruptcy Code (IBC) 2016 to speed up recovery.

LENDER RIGHTS IN LOAN AGREEMENTS

While borrowers have protections, lenders also hold certain rights to secure their interests. Such as:

1. **Right to Assess Borrower Repayment Capacity:** Lenders can evaluate a borrower's financial stability before approving a loan and reject applications if repayment ability is uncertain.
2. **Right to Charge Interest:** Lenders are entitled to charge interest on loans as per agreed terms.
3. **Right to Timely Repayment:** Borrowers must repay principal and interest as per the loan agreement.
4. **Right to Impose Reasonable Fees:** Lenders can levy processing and default fees, provided they are transparent and justified.
5. **Right to Legal Recourse in Default:** In case of default, lenders

can initiate legal proceedings, seize collateral or recover dues through court orders.

6. **Right to Assign or Sell Loan Portfolios:** Lenders may transfer loan accounts to other financial institutions or securitization companies.
7. **Right to Appoint Recovery Agents:** Lenders can engage recovery agents, but they must adhere to ethical practices and avoid harassment.

ROLE OF A LOAN GUARANTOR

A guarantor acts as a co-signer, agreeing to repay the loan if the primary borrower defaults. Lenders often require guarantors for high-value loans or when the borrower's credit worthiness is insufficient.

Key Considerations for Guarantors:

- They are legally bound to repay only if the borrower defaults.
- Missed payments by the borrower can negatively impact the guarantor's credit score.
- Before agreeing, guarantors must assess risks, as they share financial liability.

BEWARE OF FAKE LOAN APPS

With the rise of instant loan apps, fraudulent lending schemes have increased. Scammers exploit borrowers through fake apps advertised on social media, leading to financial losses and harassment.

How to Identify Fake Loan Apps:

- Lack of RBI Compliance: Legitimate lenders must follow RBI regulations and verify the lender's RBI registration.
- No Official Website: Genuine lenders have a verifiable online presence.
- No Physical Address: If it has only mobile apps/websites, but no physical address, then it should be avoided.
- Hidden Charges or No Documentation: Fraudulent apps

offer loans without requesting other necessary documents for verification.

- Negative Reviews: Check app reviews on the Play Store, Facebook or YouTube for red flags.
- Instant loan offer: Avoid apps offering 'instant loans without documents.

By staying informed and verifying lender credibility, borrowers can avoid scams and protect their financial well-being.

CHAPTER 13

UNDERSTANDING DEBT TRAPS AND CREDIT SCORES

MEANING OF DEBT TRAP

A debt trap occurs when a borrower is forced to take additional loans to repay existing ones, leading to a cycle of increasing financial obligations. This situation arises when the amount of debt to repay exceeds a borrower's income, making it difficult to break free without external intervention.

How Debt Traps Form

- Loans consist of principal (original borrowed amount) and interest (cost of borrowing).
- If EMIs are missed, penalties and compounding interest inflate the debt.
- Borrowers may take new loans to cover old ones, worsening their financial strain.

Examples of Debt Traps

1. Payday Loans – Short-term, high-interest loans that trap borrowers in a cycle of refinancing.
2. Credit Card Debt – Making minimum payments leads to accumulating interest, making repayment harder over time.
3. Job Loss or Income Drop – Sudden financial instability can make existing loans unmanageable.

Legal Consequences of Default in India

- Lenders can initiate civil lawsuits to recover dues, potentially leading to asset seizure.

- In cases of fraud or fund misappropriation, criminal charges may result in imprisonment (up to two years).
- Defaults severely damage credit scores, making future borrowing difficult.

DIFFERENTIATING BETWEEN GOOD DEBT AND BAD DEBT

Not all debt is harmful; some can be beneficial if managed wisely.

Good Debt

- Generates long-term value or income.
- Examples:
  - Home Loans (property appreciates over time)
  - Education Loans (enhances earning potential)
  - Business Loans (funds growth and revenue)

Bad Debt

- Funds depreciating or non-income-generating expenses.
- Examples:
  - Credit Card Debt (high interest for discretionary spending)
  - Personal Loans for Luxury Purchases (no return on investment)
  - Payday Loans (predatory interest rates)

AVOIDING AND MANAGING DEBT

Avoiding and managing debt involves making conscious borrowing decisions, controlling unnecessary expenses and ensuring timely repayments. It focuses on borrowing only when necessary, comparing loan terms carefully, maintaining a healthy credit score and creating a repayment plan to prevent debt from becoming a financial burden, such as:

1. **Create an Emergency Fund**: Save six months' worth of income to handle unexpected expenses without borrowing.
2. **Debt Consolidation:** Combine multiple high-interest loans into a single, lower-interest loan to simplify repayments.

3. **Track Monthly Expenses:** Identify unnecessary spending and prioritize essential payments.
4. **Follow the 40–50 per cent EMI Rule:** Ensure EMIs do not exceed 40 per cent of net income (50 per cent for home loans).
5. **Monitor Home Equity:** Regularly assess property value vs. outstanding loan to avoid negative equity risks.
6. **Prepay High-Cost Debt:** Use windfall gains (bonuses, asset sales) to clear high-interest loans first.
7. **Avoid Impulse Spending:** Differentiate between needs and wants to prevent unnecessary borrowing.

INDICATORS OF A DEBT TRAP

- Taking new loans to repay existing ones: Continuously borrowing to cover old debts is a clear sign of financial stress and unsustainable repayment capacity.
- Frequently missing EMI payment deadlines: Regularly missing EMI payment leads to late payment charges, higher interest costs and damage to credit history.
- Declining credit score due to defaults: Repeated defaults or delayed payments reduce creditworthiness, making it harder and more expensive to access future loans.
- Receiving legal notices from lenders: Legal action is often a last resort, indicating serious default and potential seizure of assets.
- Overusing credit cards for daily expenses: Depending on high-interest credit for regular needs signals a lack of sufficient income or budgeting issues.
- Spending more than monthly income: Persistent overspending without savings builds up debt quickly and leaves no room for emergencies.

CONSIDER SOME SITUATIONAL FACTORS

1. EMI-to-Salary Ratio

EMI-Salary Ratio = (Total Monthly EMIs / Monthly Income)

Example: EMI = ₹5,000

Salary = ₹15,000

Ratio = 5,000 / 15,000 = 0.33 (33%)

Recommended Limit: Below 30 per cent (0.3 ratio). So higher ratios indicate some financial stress.

2. High Personal Debt Levels

Risk Factors:

- Multiple credit cards with high balances.
- Personal loans with high interest rates.
- Struggling to pay minimum dues.

Example:

A borrower with three credit cards and two personal loans may struggle with repayment pressure due to high interest rates.

3. Lack of Financial Literacy

Consequences:

- Borrowing without understanding interest rates, penalties or repayment terms.
- Falling for predatory lending schemes (e.g., payday loans).

Example:

Taking a short-term loan at 30 per cent interest without realizing the long-term burden.

MAJOR CAUSES OF DEBT TRAPS

Debt traps often arise from excessive borrowing, poor financial planning and high-interest obligations. For example:

1. EMIs Exceeding 50 per cent of Net Income

Impact:

- Limits funds for essentials (rent, food, emergencies).

- Forces reliance on additional borrowing.

Solution:

Keep EMIs below 40–50 per cent of net income.

2. Fixed Expenses > Income

Common Triggers:

- Lifestyle inflation (luxury purchases on EMI).
- Easy loan approvals with minimal documentation.

Example:

Earning ₹30,000/month but spending ₹35,000 on EMIs + living costs.

3. Maxing Out Credit Limits

Dangers:

- Credit card interest rates (16–36 per cent p.a.).
- Minimum payments lead to compounding debt.

Solution:

Use less than 30 per cent of the credit limit to maintain a healthy score.

4. Multiple Loans without Consolidation

Problem:

Managing varied due dates and interest rates.

Fix:

Debt consolidation (single loan at a lower interest rate).

5. No Repayment Strategy

Risk:

Missing payments = Penalties + credit score damage.

Tip:

Use EMI calculators before borrowing.

CREDIT SCORES: MEANING AND IMPORTANCE

A credit score is a three-digit numerical representation (generally 300–900) of a person's credi tworthiness based on their borrowing and repayment history. It helps lenders assess the risk of lending money and influences loan approval, interest rates and credit limits. A higher score reflects responsible financial behaviour and improves access to better credit opportunities.

Different Credit Information Companies/Bureaus in India

- The CIBIL (TransUnion CIBIL): This is the most popular in this field, so CIBIL score is taken as a credit score in most places.
- Experian
- Equifax
- CRIF High Mark

HOW CREDIT SCORES WORK

A credit score is calculated by credit bureaus using information from your credit history.

Credit Report Components

1. Personal Details (Name, PAN, Address).
2. Account History (Loans, credit cards).
3. Repayment Record (On-time/late payments).
4. Credit Inquiries (Loan applications).

General Score Calculation Factors

Factor	Weightage	Impact
Payment History	35%	Late payments hurt scores.
Credit Utilization	30%	High usage (>75 per cent) lowers score.
Credit Age	15%	Older accounts improve reliability.
Credit Mix	10%	Healthy balance of secured/ unsecured loans.
New Credit	10%	Too many applications reduce scores.

Good vs Bad Scores

CIBIL Score	Meaning	Impact on Borrowing
750 – 900	Excellent	Very high approval chances with the best interest rates
700 – 749	Good	Good approval chances with competitive rates
650 – 699	Fair	Moderate approval chances, interest rates may be higher
550 – 649	Poor	Low approval chances, loans available at high interest rates
300 – 549	Very Poor	Very low approval chances, high risk for lenders

- CIBIL is the most widely used.
- No credit history? Score shows -1 (no data which means never taking a loan).
- 0 (<6 months history).
- Generally, it needs 18–36-month credit history.

Why Credit Scores Matter

- Loan Approvals – Higher scores increase approval chances.
- Interest Rates – Better scores secure lower rates.
- Employment and Rentals – Though it is not mandatory, some employers/landlords also check credit history to select employees/tenants.

FINANCIAL RISKS, FRAUDS AND PROTECTION

CHAPTER 14

FINANCIAL MIS-SELLING – RISKS, PREVENTION AND REMEDIES

UNDERSTANDING FINANCIAL MIS-SELLING

Financial mis-selling happens when a financial product is sold based on false information, hiding important facts or the recommending of a product that is unsuitable for the customer's needs or risk profile. This can lead to financial loss, disappointment and loss of trust in financial institutions. It often occurs in products like insurance, mutual funds, loans or investment schemes where customers may not fully understand the terms, risks or charges.

COMMON EXAMPLES IN INDIA :

1. Insurance Sold as Fixed Deposits

- Tactic: Bank staff push regular-premium insurance policies disguised as 'better-return FDs' to senior citizens.
- Impact: Policyholders discover later that they must pay annual premiums, often under their children's names.

2. Lumpsum Premiums Masked as Single Payments

- Tactic: Agents sell multiple policies under the guise of a 'one-time payment' plan.
- Impact: Customers receive renewal notices after a year, realizing they were misled.

3. Misleading Net Asset Value (NAV) Guarantees in Mutual Funds

- **Tactic:** Promising 'highest NAV' returns without clarifying market risks.
- **Red Flag:** Fine print excludes liability for market downturns.

LEGAL RECOURSE FOR VICTIMS

Victims of financial mis-selling can approach consumer courts, banking ombudsman offices or regulatory authorities such as SEBI and IRDAI to seek justice. These bodies can order compensation, cancel fraudulent contracts and impose penalties on the offenders.

- **Grounds for Complaint:**
    - Material misrepresentation (false claims).
    - Suitability violation (product mismatched to needs).
- **Steps to Take:**
    - Gather evidence (policy documents, recorded calls, emails).
    - File a complaint with the institution's grievance cell.

1. Escalate to regulators (RBI, IRDAI, SEBI) or the banking ombudsman.
    - Legal action – if any monetary losses (Consumer Court) or for fraud(civil/criminal suit).

CONSEQUENCES OF MIS-SELLING

Financial mis-selling can lead to monetary losses, unmet financial goals and loss of trust in financial institutions. It may also result in legal disputes and long-term damage to an investor's financial security.

For Customers

- Financial Losses: Unsuitable investments or policies erode savings.
- Credit Damage: Missed premiums/EMIs hurt credit scores.
- Eroded Trust: Scepticism towards banks/insurers.

For Institutions

- Regulatory Penalties: Fines by RBI/IRDAI
- Reputation Risk: Public scandals
- Legal Costs: Compensation payouts and litigation expenses.

HOW FINANCIAL INSTITUTIONS CAN PREVENT MIS-SELLING

1. Transparency and Ethics

- Disclose all risks, fees and lock-in periods upfront.
- Ban incentives for selling high-commission products.

2. Employee Training

- Train staff on:
  - Product suitability (e.g., not selling equity-linked plans to risk-averse retirees).
  - Ethical selling (no pressure tactics).

3. Robust Compliance

- Pre-sale checks: Verify customer's income, goals and risk appetite.
- Audits: Randomly review sales call and paperwork.

4. Customer Redressal

- Resolve complaints within 30 days (RBI mandate).
- Offer refunds or policy adjustments for proven mis-selling.

GUIDELINES FOR CUSTOMERS: HOW TO AVOID MIS-SELLING

Customers can avoid mis-selling by verifying product details, understanding terms and risks and dealing only with authorized agents or institutions. Asking questions and keeping written records of all communications adds further protection. Such as:

1. Ask Critical Questions

- Is this product regulated by RBI/IRDAI/SEBI?
- What are the surrender charges if I exit early?

- Can you show me a comparison with similar products?

2. Verify Too-Good-Be-True Claims

- Reject promises like:
  - Guaranteed 15 per cent returns (market-linked returns are never guaranteed).
  - No medical tests for health insurance (may lead to claim rejection).

3. Read the Fine Print

- Check for:
  - Hidden fees (e.g., premium allocation charges in ULIPs).
  - Lock-in periods (e.g., three years in equity-linked savings schemes).

4. Avoid High-Pressure Sales

- Walk away if agents say:
  - Offer valid only today.
  - Your FD will earn less than this policy.

5. Use Regulatory Safeguards

- Free-Look Period: Cancel insurance policies within 15 days (30 days for online or distance purchase) to receive a refund after permissible deductions.
- Cooling-Off Clause: Exit mutual funds within five days with minimal penalties.

CHAPTER 15

FINANCIAL FRAUD

In recent years, the adoption of digital payment methods has surged, particularly during the COVID-19 pandemic, when lockdowns accelerated the shift towards cashless transactions. While this transition has enhanced convenience and advanced financial inclusion, it has also led to an increase in financial fraud. Fraudsters continuously devise new and sophisticated techniques to exploit common men, particularly those new to digital platforms who may not fully understand the risks involved.

Financial fraud refers to deceptive or illegal activities aimed at depriving individuals or organizations of their money, assets or financial security. It involves intentional misrepresentation, concealment of facts or manipulation of financial transactions for unlawful personal gain.

Key characteristics of financial fraud include:

- Deceptive Practices: Fraudsters use false pretences to trick victims into surrendering money or sensitive information.
- Illegal Gain: The primary motive is personal enrichment at the expense of the victim.
- Abuse of Trust: Many frauds involve exploiting a position of trust, such as impersonating bank officials or government representatives.
- Misrepresentation: Fraudulent schemes often involve falsified

documents, fake investment opportunities or manipulated financial records.

Financial fraud can take many forms, ranging from identity theft to complex Ponzi schemes. Understanding these fraud types is crucial to safeguarding oneself against financial crimes.

COMMON TYPES OF FINANCIAL FRAUD

1. Ponzi Schemes

A Ponzi scheme is an investment scam where returns are paid to earlier investors using funds collected from new investors, rather than from legitimate profits. The scheme collapses when the flow of new investors slows down, leaving most participants with significant losses.

How It Works:

- Fraudsters promise unusually high returns with minimal risk.
- Initial investors receive payouts to build credibility, attracting more victims.
- No real investment occurs; money from new investors is used to pay earlier ones.
- The scheme collapses when new investments dry up.

Warning Signs:

- Guaranteed high returns with no risk (all investments carry some risk).
- Overly consistent profits (legitimate investments fluctuate).
- Unregistered investments or unlicenced sellers (always verify regulatory compliance).
- Difficulty withdrawing funds (fraudsters discourage withdrawals to sustain the scam).

2. Pyramid Schemes

A pyramid scheme operates by recruiting members who pay to join, with earnings tied to enrolling others rather than selling actual products. These schemes inevitably collapse when recruitment becomes unsustainable.

Charles Ponzi's 1920's postal coupon scam, where he swindled millions by promising impossible returns, gave this fraud its name.

Ponzi ran a scheme in the United States promising huge returns from postage stamp trading. His scam collapsed within a year, costing investors millions of dollars.

How It Works:

- Participants pay an entry fee and earn commissions by recruiting others.
- No genuine product or service is sold; profits come solely from new recruits.
- The scheme collapses when recruitment stalls, leaving most participants with losses.

The SpeakAsia scam was one of India's largest online Ponzi-style frauds. The company claimed to be a Singapore-based online survey business and lured people with promises of high returns for completing simple online surveys. Investors had to pay a membership fee to join, after which they were told they would earn income by filling out surveys and recruiting more members. Instead of generating revenue from legitimate business activities, SpeakAsia used funds from new members to pay returns to existing ones, following the classic Ponzi model. When new enrolments slowed, the scheme collapsed.

Over 24 lakh investors across India lost approximately ₹2,276 crore, leading to multiple investigations by the Economic Offences Wing

(EOW), Enforcement Directorate (ED) and Serious Fraud Investigation Office (SFIO). The case highlighted the need for stronger regulation of online investment schemes.

3. Identity Theft and Identity Fraud

Identity thefts occur when someone steals personal information (e.g., bank details, Aadhaar, PAN) to commit fraud. Identity fraud involves using stolen data to impersonate the victim for financial gain.

Common Methods:

- Shoulder surfing (observing PIN entries in public)
- Phishing emails/SMS scams (fake links requesting personal details)
- Malware attacks (stealing data via infected software)
- Social media exploitation (guessing passwords from public posts)

Consequences:

- Unauthorized bank withdrawals
- Fraudulent loans/credit cards opened in the victim's name
- Legal troubles if the stolen identity is used for criminal activities

4. Credit Card Fraud

Unauthorized use of a credit/debit card to make purchases or withdraw funds.

Common Tactics:

- Skimming: Installing devices on ATMs to steal card data.
- Phishing: Tricking victims into revealing card details via fake calls/emails.
- Card not in hand fraud: Using stolen card details for online transactions.

Prevention:

- Regularly monitor bank statements
- Report lost/stolen cards immediately
- Avoid sharing CVV/OTP with anyone

5. KYC Fraud / Vishing Calls (Voice Phishing)

Fraudsters impersonate as bank officials, claiming the victim's account will be blocked unless they 'update KYC'. They extract sensitive details (OTP, PIN, CVV) to steal money.

How It Works:

- Victims receive fake calls/SMS demanding urgent KYC updates.
- Fraudsters trick them into sharing login credentials or installing remote-access apps.
- Funds are siphoned off once access is gained.

Prevention:

- Banks never ask for sensitive details via call/SMS.
- Verify requests by contacting the bank directly.
- Never install unknown apps suggested by callers.

6. Phishing Attacks

Fraudsters create fake websites/emails mimicking legitimate institutions to steal login credentials.

Common Techniques:

- Link manipulation: Fake URLs leading to fraudulent sites.
- Smishing/Vishing: Fraudulent SMS/calls requesting personal data.
- Malware-infected attachments: Installing spyware via email downloads.

Protection Measures:

- Check sender email addresses for authenticity.
- Avoid clicking on suspicious links.
- Enable two-factor authentication (2FA).

7. Money Mule Scams

Victims are tricked into laundering illegal money through their bank accounts, often under the guise of 'easy money' job offers.

How It Works:

- Fraudsters offer commissions for receiving/transferring money.
- Victims unknowingly facilitate illegal transactions.
- When authorities investigate, the money mule faces legal consequences.

Prevention:

- Reject unsolicited money transfer offers.
- Verify job offers thoroughly before accepting.

8. Online Sales Platform Frauds

Scammers pose as buyers on platforms like OLX, tricking sellers into authorizing UPI 'request money' links instead of receiving payments.

Common Tactics:

- Fake buyers claiming to be defence personnel.
- Sellers are tricked into entering their UPI PIN, leading to unauthorized debits.

Prevention:

- Never share UPI PIN for receiving money.
- Verify buyer authenticity before transactions.

9. Advance Fee Scams

Fraudsters demand upfront payments for fake rewards, loans or lottery winnings.

Examples:

- Lottery scams: Victims pay 'processing fees' for non-existent prizes.
- Loan scams: Fraudsters ask for advance payments before approving loans.

Prevention:

- Never pay upfront for promised rewards.
- Verify offers through official channels.

10. ATM Skimming

Fraudsters install hidden devices on ATMs to clone card data and steal PINs via cameras.

Protection Tips:

- Inspect ATMs for suspicious attachments.
- Shield the keypad while entering PINs.

11. UPI-Related Frauds

Fraudsters send fake 'request money' links or malware-infected URLs to steal financial data.

Prevention:

- Avoid clicking on unknown UPI links.
- Use verified UPI handles only.

12. Deepfake Investment Scams

AI-generated fake videos of celebrities or experts promoting fraudulent investment schemes.

Prevention:

- Cross-check investment tips on SEBI's website.
- Report suspicious content to authorities.

13. Digital Arrest Scams

Scammers impersonate law enforcement, threatening arrest unless victims pay fines or share personal details.

Prevention:

- No legal authority conducts arrests over calls.
- Report such calls to cybercrime authorities immediately.

COMPREHENSIVE GUIDE TO PROTECTING YOURSELF FROM FINANCIAL FRAUD

Financial fraud is a growing threat in today's digital world, with scammers employing increasingly sophisticated tactics to exploit unsuspecting individuals. Protecting yourself requires vigilance, awareness and proactive security measures. Below is an extensive list of best practices to safeguard your finances and personal information from fraudsters.

1. Beware of Shoulder Surfing

Shoulder surfing occurs when a fraudster observes you entering sensitive information, such as your ATM PIN or online banking credentials, by looking over your shoulder. It is particularly common in crowded places like ATMs, retail stores or public transport.

Prevention Tips:

- Shield the keypad when entering your PIN at ATMs or point-of-sale terminals.
- Avoid typing passwords or PINs in public view.

- Be cautious of strangers standing too close while you conduct financial transactions.

2. Educate Yourself on Common Scams

Knowledge is your strongest defence against fraud. Stay updated on the latest scams by:

- Following alerts from banks, the RBI and cybercrime authorities.
- Reading financial fraud advisories from government websites.
- Participating in financial literacy programmes.

3. Verify Identities Before Sharing Information

Fraudsters often impersonate bank officials, government agents or customer service representatives to extract sensitive details.

Red Flags:

- Unsolicited calls/SMS asking for OTP, PIN or CVV.
- Emails requesting urgent account updates.
- Callers threatening account blockage or legal action unless you comply.

Best Practices:

- Never share OTPs, passwords or PINs over calls or messages.
- Contact the institution directly using official numbers (not from Google search results).
- Hang up immediately if a caller pressures you for information.

4. Use Strong and Unique Passwords

Weak passwords make accounts vulnerable to hacking.

Password Security Tips:

- Use at least 12 characters with a mix of letters, numbers and symbols.
- Avoid common words, birthdays or sequential numbers.
- Change passwords periodically and never reuse them across accounts.
- Consider a password manager for secure storage.

5. Enable Two-Factor Authentication (2FA)

2FA adds an extra security layer by requiring a second verification step (e.g., OTP, biometric scan).

Where to Enable 2FA:

- Banking apps
- Email accounts
- UPI and digital wallets

6. Be Cautious with Emails (Phishing Scams)

Fraudulent emails mimic legitimate institutions to trick victims into revealing login credentials.

How to Spot Phishing Emails:

Check sender's email address (look for misspellings like 'support@bankk.com').

Be careful. Hover over links (don't click, verify the URL first). Look for poor grammar or urgency ('Your account will be blocked in 24 hours!').

Protection Measures:

- Never download attachments from unknown senders.
- Report phishing emails to your bank or cybercrime authorities.

7. Beware of Fraudulent Phone Calls (Vishing)

Scammers impersonate bank representatives, tax officials or tech support to extract sensitive data.

Prevention Steps:

- Do not share OTPs, CVV or login details over calls.
- Verify callers independently by contacting the official helpline.
- Register for 'Do Not Disturb (DND)' to reduce spam calls.

8. Secure Your Devices

Malware and spyware can steal financial data from infected devices.

Security Measures:

- Install reputable antivirus software and update it regularly.
- Enable automatic OS and app updates to patch security flaws.
- Avoid sideloading apps from unknown sources.
- Use separate user accounts for work and personal use.

9. Avoid Public Wi-Fi for Financial Transactions

Public Wi-Fi networks are often insecure, making them hotspots for data theft.

Safe Alternatives:

- Use mobile data or a trusted VPN for secure browsing.
- Never log into banking apps on open networks.

10. Monitor Bank and Credit Card Statements Regularly

Early detection of unauthorized transactions can prevent major losses.

What to Do:

- Check statements weekly for unfamiliar debits.
- Report suspicious transactions immediately to your bank.
- Enable SMS/email alerts for all transactions.

11. Research Before Investing

Fraudulent investment schemes promise high returns with little risk.

Warning Signs:

- Guaranteed high returns with no risk.
- Pressure to invest quickly ('Limited-time offer!').
- Unregistered brokers or firms (verify on SEBI's website).

Prevention:

- Consult a SEBI-registered advisor before investing.
- Avoid unsolicited stock tips via WhatsApp or social media.

12. Report Suspicious Activity Immediately

If you suspect fraud, act fast to minimize damage.

Where to Report in India:

- Local police cybercrime cell
- National Cyber Crime Portal (https://cybercrime.gov.in)
- RBI Ombudsman

13. Stay Informed About New Scams

Fraud tactics evolve constantly. Stay updated via:

- RBI alerts
- Bank notifications
- News reports on financial scams

14. Seek Legal Advice if Defrauded

If you fall victim to fraud:

- File an FIR with the local police.

- Consult a lawyer for recovery options.
- Notify your bank to freeze compromised accounts.

15. Never Share OTPs or Financial Details

- OTPs are for your eyes only; never share them, even with 'bank officials'.
- Avoid posting financial details on social media (e.g., card screenshots).

16. Deposit Money Only in Authorized Institutions

Avoid unauthorized agents offering 'higher interest' schemes.

- Verify bank/financial institution legitimacy via RBI's website.
- Never hand over cash to middlemen for deposits.

17. Use Secure Payment Gateways

When shopping online:

- Look for 'https://' and padlock icons in the URL.
- Enter CVV only on trusted sites (avoid saving card details).

18. Read Financial Contracts Carefully

Before signing:

- Review terms and conditions (watch for hidden charges).
- Avoid signing blank forms or incomplete documents.

19. Ignore Spam Emails and Fake Lottery Scams

- No legitimate lottery asks for upfront fees.
- Delete unsolicited reward emails without responding.

20. Remember: Banks Never Ask for Confidential Data

- No genuine entity requests passwords, PINs or OTPs.
- Hang up and report if someone demands such details.

21. Install Trusted Antivirus Software

Protect all devices with:

- Real-time malware scanning.
- Firewall protection.

REGULATION AND GRIEVANCE REDRESSAL

CHAPTER 16

FINANCIAL REGULATORY BODIES IN INDIA

India's financial system is a vast and intricate network that includes banking, capital markets, insurance, mutual funds, pension funds and corporate governance. To ensure stability, transparency and fairness in these sectors, the government has established several financial regulatory bodies. These institutions act as watchdogs, enforcing rules, preventing malpractices and protecting the interests of consumers, investors and businesses.

Key Objectives of Financial Regulators in India

1. Financial Stability – Ensuring the smooth functioning of financial markets and preventing systemic risks.
2. Consumer Protection – Safeguarding the rights of investors, policyholders and depositors.
3. Market Confidence – Maintaining trust in financial institutions and markets.
4. Reduction in Financial Crimes – Preventing fraud, scams and unethical financial practices.

MAJOR FINANCIAL REGULATORY BODIES IN INDIA

Financial regulatory bodies such as the RBI, SEBI, IRDAI and Pension Fund Regulatory and Development Authority (PFRDA) oversee and regulate different segments of the financial system to ensure stability, transparency and investor protection.

1. Reserve Bank of India (RBI)

The RBI is India's central banking institution, responsible for monetary policy, currency issuance and banking regulation.

Key Functions:

- Monetary Policy Regulation – Controls inflation and liquidity through repo rate, Cash Reserve Ratio (CRR) and Statutory Liquidity Ratio (SLR) adjustments.
- Banking Supervision – Licences and regulates commercial banks, NBFCs and payment systems.
- Currency Management – Issues and circulates currency notes.
- Financial Stability – Acts as a lender of last resort during economic crises.
- Consumer Protection – Ensures fair banking practices and grievance redressal.

(Note: A detailed discussion on RBI is covered in Chapter 1.)

2. Securities and Exchange Board of India (SEBI)

SEBI is the apex regulator of India's securities and capital markets, ensuring transparency, fairness and investor protection.

Key Functions:

- Regulates Stock Exchanges – Oversees BSE, NSE and other exchanges.
- Supervises Market Intermediaries – Brokers, mutual funds, portfolio managers.
- Prevents Insider Trading & Fraud – Enforces strict penalties for market manipulation.
- Investor Education – Promotes financial literacy and awareness.
- Corporate Governance – Monitors mergers, acquisitions and corporate disclosures.

Major Achievements:

- Introduction of the T+1 settlement cycle for faster trade settlements.
- Strict regulations against Ponzi schemes and illegal investment platforms.

Settlement Cycles

- **T+0** – Trade and settlement happen on the same day.
- **T+1** – Settlement occurs one business day after the trade date (currently used in India for equities). In India, the T+1 settlement cycle was fully implemented in January 2023 to make transactions faster and reduce settlement risk.
- **T+2** – Settlement occurs two business days after the trade date (was the standard before T+1 in India).
- For example, if you buy shares on Monday, the transfer of shares to your account and payment to the seller will happen by Tuesday (assuming both days are working days).

3. Insurance Regulatory and Development Authority of India (IRDAI)

IRDAI regulates and promotes the insurance sector, ensuring policyholder protection and industry growth.

Key Functions:

- Licenses Insurers – Approves new insurance companies and products.
- Regulates Premiums and Policies – Ensures fair pricing and terms.
- Claims Settlement Oversight – Mandates the timely processing of claims.
- Consumer Grievance Redressal – Handles complaints against insurers.

Recent Initiatives:

- Bima Sugam – A digital marketplace for insurance policies.
- Standardization of health insurance terms.

4. Pension Funds Regulatory and Development Authority (PFRDA)

PFRDA governs India's pension sector, primarily overseeing the NPS.

Key Functions:

- Regulates Pension Fund Managers – Ensures compliance with investment norms.
- Protects Subscriber Interests – Monitors fund performance and transparency.
- Promotes Retirement Planning – Spreads awareness about pension schemes.

Major Schemes:

- National Pension System (NPS) – A voluntary, long-term retirement savings scheme.
- Atal Pension Yojana (APY) – A government-backed pension scheme for the unorganized sector.

5. Ministry of Corporate Affairs (MCA)

The MCA regulates corporate entities, ensuring compliance with the Companies Act, 2013 and other corporate laws.

Key Functions:

- Company Incorporation and Compliance – Oversees the Registrar of Companies (RoC).
- Corporate Governance Enforcement – Ensures transparency in financial reporting.
- Insolvency & Bankruptcy Regulation – Manages the Insolvency and Bankruptcy Code (IBC).
- Investor Protection – Handles grievances against fraudulent companies.

Recent Reforms:

- Simplification of corporate compliance for startups.
- Stricter penalties for financial frauds like shell company scams.

OTHER IMPORTANT FINANCIAL BODIES

Association of Mutual Funds in India (AMFI)

AMFI is a self-regulatory, non-statutory body that promotes ethical practices in the mutual fund industry.

Key Roles:

- Regulatory Compliance – Ensures Asset Management Companies (AMCs) follow SEBI guidelines.
- Investor Awareness – Educates the public about mutual fund investments.
- NAV Publication – Mandates daily disclosure of NAV.
- Code of Conduct – Enforces ethical standards among members.

Major Contributions:

- Mutual Fund Sahi Hai Campaign – Increased retail participation in mutual funds.
- Standardization of KYC norms for investors.

CHAPTER 17

OMBUDSMAN AND GRIEVANCE REDRESSAL PLATFORMS IN INDIA

INTRODUCTION TO THE OMBUDSMAN SYSTEM

In any financial system, customers and investors may face issues such as unfair practices, service deficiencies or fraudulent activities by financial institutions. To address these grievances effectively, India has established Ombudsman schemes, which are independent and impartial authorities that mediate between consumers and financial service providers. An Ombudsman is an official appointed to investigate and resolve complaints against administrative authorities or financial entities.

Their role includes:

- Ensuring fair treatment of consumers.
- Providing a cost-free and efficient dispute resolution mechanism.
- Identifying systemic issues in financial services that need reform.

India has specialized Ombudsman mechanisms and a grievance platform for different financial sectors, including:

1. RBI's Integrated Ombudsman Scheme (RB-IOS, 2021) – For banking, NBFCs and digital transactions.
2. Insurance Ombudsman – For insurance-related grievances.
3. SEBI's SCORES Portal – For capital market complaints.

This chapter explores these mechanisms, including how to file complaints, eligibility criteria and resolution processes.

RESERVE BANK'S INTEGRATED OMBUDSMAN SCHEME (RBI-IOS, 2021)

Overview

The RBI merged three earlier Ombudsman schemes into a unified system under the RBI-IOS, 2021, to streamline grievance redressal. The integrated scheme covers customers of the following Regulated Entities (REs):

- Banks (Public, Private, Foreign, Co-operative)
- Non-Banking Financial Companies (NBFCs)
- Payment System Participant (PSPs)
- Credit Information Companies (CICs)

Key Features of RBI-IOS, 2021

- Based on the principle of One Nation, One Ombudsman with jurisdiction-neutral complaint handling.
- No monetary limit on the value of disputes, though compensation is capped at ₹20 lakh.
- Provides free and time-bound resolution, with regulated entities required to respond within 30 days.
- Covers a wide range of services including digital transactions, loans and banking operations.

WHAT IS A DEFICIENCY IN SERVICE?

Under the scheme, a 'deficiency in service' refers to:

- Failure to provide a promised financial service.
- Unfair practices (hidden charges, wrongful debits).
- Delays or refusals in resolving complaints.
- Mis-selling of financial products.

PROCEDURE FOR FILING A COMPLAINT

Step 1: Approach the Regulated Entity (RE)

Before approaching the Ombudsman, a complainant must first file a written complaint with the concerned bank or NBFC. If the regulated

entity fails to respond within 30 days or gives an unsatisfactory reply, the customer can then escalate the matter to the RBI Ombudsman.

Step 2: Submit a Complaint to the RBI Ombudsman

Complaints can be filed via:

Online Portal – CMS Portal (https://cms.rbi.org.in)

Email – Send details to crpc@rbi.org.in

Physical Complaint – Send via post to:

Centralized Receipt and Processing Centre (CRPC),
4th Floor, Reserve Bank of India,
Sector-17, Central Vista, Chandigarh – 160017

MANDATORY DETAILS REQUIRED

- Complainant's name, address, email and mobile number.
- Bank/NBFC branch details (where the issue occurred).
- Transaction details (account number, date, amount).
- Previous complaint reference (if already raised with the bank).
- Nature of loss and relief sought.
- Supporting documents (bank statements, emails, etc.).

MONETARY COMPENSATION LIMITS

- There is no upper limit on the disputed transaction amount.
- Maximum compensation for financial loss is capped at ₹20 lakh.
- An additional compensation of up to ₹1 lakh may be awarded for mental harassment.

EXCLUSIONS (COMPLAINTS NOT COVERED)

- Commercial decisions (e.g., loan rejection).
- Pending court cases.
- Complaints older than 1 year (from RE's reply date).
- Employee-related disputes.

HELPLINE AND SUPPORT

- Toll-Free Number: 14448 (24x7 IVRS support).
- Live Agent Support: 8 a.m. - 10 p.m. (Weekdays, in English/Hindi).
- Regional Language Support: 9:30 a.m. –5:15 p.m. (10 languages).

INSURANCE OMBUDSMAN (IRDAI GRIEVANCE REDRESSAL)

Overview

The IO is an independent authority set up to resolve disputes between policyholders and insurance companies fairly and impartially. It was established under the Redressal of Public Grievances Rules, 1998, framed by the Government of India to provide policyholders with an affordable and accessible forum for resolving complaints. Unlike lengthy court processes, the Ombudsman provides a cost-free and time-bound mechanism for resolution, thereby ensuring policyholders' interests are protected and confidence in the insurance sector is strengthened.

Who Can File a Complaint?

- Individual policyholders.
- Nominees/legal heirs.
- Complaints related to claim delays, rejections and mis-selling.

PROCEDURE FOR FILING A COMPLAINT

Step 1: Approach the Insurance Company First

- Complain in writing to the insurer's grievance cell.
- If unresolved within 30 days, escalate to the Ombudsman.

Step 2: Submit to the Insurance Ombudsman

Online: visiting website of the Council of Insurance Ombudsman (www.cioins.co.in)

- Offline: Submit a physical complaint to the nearest Ombudsman Office (17 locations in India), which is under Council for Insurance Ombudsman (CIO).

Required Details

- Policy number, claim details, insurer's response.
- Copies of policy documents, claim rejection letters.

Time Limit

- Must be filed within one year of insurer's reply.

Compensation Limit

- Maximum ₹50 lakh

RBI OMBUDSMAN PROCESS

When a complaint is submitted to the RBI Ombudsman, it undergoes a preliminary review to determine whether it falls within the scope of maintainable grievances. If the complaint is found to be non-maintainable, it is formally closed and the complainant is informed of the decision with appropriate reasoning.

For maintainable complaints, the Ombudsman facilitates a resolution through mutual agreement between the complainant and the RE, typically a bank or financial institution. If both parties reach an amicable settlement, the terms are documented in a written agreement signed by both sides. Since the resolution is mutually accepted, the Ombudsman does not issue a formal award and the settlement becomes binding. However, if the dispute remains unresolved despite mediation efforts, the Ombudsman proceeds with a formal adjudication. After evaluating the evidence, applicable banking laws, RBI guidelines and other relevant factors, the Ombudsman may either:

- Issue an Award, directing the RE to take corrective action (such as compensation or rectification of service deficiencies) or
- Reject the complaint if the RE is to be found compliant with regulatory norms.

The final decision is communicated to both the complainant and the RE, ensuring transparency in the grievance redressal process.

Insurance Ombudsman Process (IO)

The IO serves as an alternative dispute resolution mechanism for policyholders dissatisfied with their insurer's response. Established by the government, this system ensures impartial, cost-effective and expedited resolutions without requiring litigation.

Scope of Complaints

The Insurance Ombudsman addresses grievances related to:

1. Delayed claim settlements
2. Partial or complete claim rejections
3. Disputes over premium calculations
4. Misrepresentation of policy terms
5. Legal interpretation of policy clauses
6. Policy servicing issues (including agent/intermediary misconduct)
7. Discrepancies between policy documents and proposal forms
8. Non-issuance of policies after premium payment
9. Violations of IRDAI regulations

Pre-complaint Requirements

Before approaching the IO, the policyholder must:

- First lodge a complaint with the insurer or broker and either receive an unsatisfactory response or no reply within 30 days.
- Ensure the complaint is filed within one year of the insurer's rejection or the expiry of the 30-day response period.
- Limit the compensation sought to ₹50 lakhs.
- Confirm that the matter is not already subjudice in court or a consumer forum, etc.

Complaint Submission

Complaints can be submitted:

- Online (via email or dedicated portals)
- Offline (by post or in-person at an IO office)

Resolution Process

1. Registration and Documentation: The IO verifies the complaint, along with supporting documents (policy copies, correspondence with the insurer).
2. Insurer's Response: The insurer is required to submit its defence.

3. Hearing: The IO conducts hearings (primarily online since 2021, though in-person options remain available for those with connectivity issues).

Outcomes

- Settlement (Recommendation under Rule 16) – If both parties agree to a fair resolution, it is formalized as a binding recommendation.
- Merit-Based Award (Rule 17) – If no settlement is reached, the IO issues a binding decision on the insurer. While the insurer cannot appeal, the complainant retains the right to pursue further legal action.

The amended 2021 IO rules have streamlined the process by enabling digital filings and virtual hearings, enhancing accessibility while maintaining procedural rigour. Despite the convenience of online submissions, many complainants still prefer physical filings, which are treated with equal priority.

Both the RBI and IO frameworks emphasize fairness, efficiency and adherence to regulatory standards, ensuring that consumers have accessible avenues for dispute resolution without protracted legal battles.

SEBI COMPLAINTS REDRESS SYSTEM (SCORES) – A DETAILED OVERVIEW

The SEBI has established SCORES, a centralized, web-based platform designed to facilitate the resolution of investor grievances related to the securities market. This system ensures that investors who have not received satisfactory resolutions from listed companies, brokers or other registered intermediaries can escalate their complaints for further action.

Purpose of SCORES

SCORES serves as an online grievance redressal mechanism for investors facing unresolved issues with:

- Listed companies
- SEBI-registered intermediaries (such as brokers, mutual funds and depository participants)
- Market Infrastructure Institutions (like stock exchanges and depositories)

Before approaching SCORES, investors must first attempt to resolve their complaints directly with the concerned entity (company, broker or exchange). Only if the issue remains unresolved or no response is received can the investor escalate the matter to SCORES.

Types of Complaints Covered Under SCORES

SCORES addresses grievances arising from violations or deficiencies under:

- The SEBI Act, 1992
- The Securities Contracts (Regulation) Act, 1956
- The Depositories Act, 1996
- Relevant provisions of the Companies Act, 2013 (as administered by SEBI)

Complaints NOT Considered Under SCORES

Certain matters fall outside the scope of SCORES and will not be entertained, including:

- Complaints not related to securities markets or investments in securities.
- Anonymous complaints are not accepted because identity verification is mandatory.
- Vague or incomplete complaints that lack specific details.
- Allegations made without supporting documents.
- General suggestions or requests for guidance that do not qualify as grievances.
- Dissatisfaction with share prices, which should be raised through the Market Intermediaries Portal.
- Non-listing of private placement shares, unless there is a violation of securities laws.

- Private contractual disputes that are outside the purview of SEBI regulations.
- Cases involving fake or forged documents must be reported to legal authorities.
- Complaints against unlisted or delisted companies.
- Matters falling under the jurisdiction of other regulators, such as RBI, IRDAI, PFRDA or CCI.
- Unregistered or unregulated financial activities.
- Cases already pending in courts or under arbitration

Time Limit for Filing Complaints

To ensure efficient resolution, complaints must be lodged on SCORES within one year from the date of the incident causing the grievance. SEBI may reject complaints filed after this period.

KYC Requirements

For filing a complaint on SCORES, investors must provide the following mandatory details:

- Full Name
- Address
- Email Address
- PAN
- Mobile Number
- Date of Birth

Upon submission, a unique registration number is generated for tracking the complaint. An acknowledgment email is also sent to the registered email ID.

Checking Complaint Status

Investors can monitor their complaint status by:

- Logging into their SCORES account
- Using the registration number and password (for physical complaints, the password is provided in SEBI's acknowledgment letter)

Best Practices Before Using SCORES

SCORES is a transparent, efficient and investor-friendly platform designed to expedite grievance resolution in the securities market. By adhering to SEBI's guidelines and providing accurate details, investors can effectively escalate unresolved issues and seek redressal. However, direct communication with the concerned entity remains the first step towards resolution, ensuring faster and more amicable settlements wherever possible.

Before filing a complaint on SCORES, investors should:

1. First approach the concerned entity (broker, company or exchange) for resolution.
2. Retain all communication records (emails, letters, transaction proofs) as supporting evidence.
3. Ensure the complaint is clear, specific and well-documented to avoid rejection.

Choosing the Right Redressal Mechanism

Grievance Type	Platform	Contact Method	Compensation Limit
Banking/ NBFC Issues	RBI Ombudsman (RBI-IOS)	CMS Portal / 14448 Helpline	₹20 lakh + ₹1 lakh (mental harassment)
Insurance Disputes	Insurance Ombudsman	Online/ Offline Submission	₹50 lakh
Stock Market Issues	SEBI SCORES	Online (https://scores.sebi.gov.in/)	Case-specific

LEGACY AND
ESTATE PLANNING

CHAPTER 18

ESSENTIALS OF ESTATE AND PROPERTY PLANNING

Estate or property planning involves systematically organizing and allocating one's assets during their lifetime to ensure a smooth transfer to beneficiaries such as family members, dependents or institutions after their death. Effective estate planning not only ensures that assets are distributed according to the individual's wishes but also helps reduce legal complications, family disputes and unnecessary costs such as excessive taxation or lengthy court procedures.

KEY COMPONENT OF ESTATE PLANNING: WILL (TESTAMENTARY DOCUMENT)

A Will is a legally recognized document that specifies how an individual's assets, including property, investments and personal belongings, should be distributed after death. It provides certainty, prevents confusion and reduces the likelihood of conflicts among heirs. A properly drafted Will ensures that the deceased's wishes are respected and legally enforced. It may also include the appointment of an executor, who is responsible for carrying out the instructions mentioned in the Will. In India, while registration of a Will is not mandatory, registering it adds an additional layer of authenticity and reduces the chances of disputes.

Key Considerations When Drafting a Will

- List all movable and immovable assets (property, bank accounts, investments, jewelry, etc.).
- Specify beneficiaries for each asset (partial or complete allocation).

- Appoint an executor (a trusted person responsible for executing the Will).
- Witnesses (preferably a doctor and a lawyer) add legal validity.
- Registration (optional but recommended for authenticity).
- Can be handwritten or drafted with legal assistance (plain paper suffices, but legal guidance ensures compliance).

Consequences of Not Having a Will

- Distribution follows personal/succession laws, which may not align with the deceased's wishes.
- Legal disputes among heirs can lead to prolonged litigation.
- Higher costs in asset transfer due to court procedures.
- Delays in inheritance settlement (sometimes taking years).

Challenge against Will

You cannot include in your Will any portion of property that is not self-acquired, such as ancestral or joint family property. If you attempt to do so, that part of the Will becomes invalid and is treated as void.

In that sense, Will is not the last word; it can also be challenged in court. Generally, a dissatisfied legal heir files a case against the Will. In the following situation, it can be challenged:

i) made by a minor
ii) if the signature is forged
iii) if it is made not in the normal state of health of that person
iv) undue influence, coercion applied at the time of making the Will
v) not clear; ambiguity or uncertainty in the Will

2. NOMINATION (CUSTODIAL RIGHT, NOT OWNERSHIP)

A nominee is a temporary custodian appointed to hold and transfer assets to legal heirs after the owner's death. Nomination does not grant ownership rights.

Why Nomination is Important

- Simplifies asset transfer (avoids lengthy legal processes).

- Mandatory in some cases (bank accounts, mutual funds, insurance).
- Acts as a safeguard until legal heirs claim the assets.

Example Scenario

- Suresh nominates Ramesh for his bank FD.
- Upon Suresh's death, Ramesh receives the funds but must transfer them to Suresh's legal heirs.
- If Ramesh refuses, heirs must file a legal claim.

NOMINEE VS. LEGAL HEIR

People often confuse nominees with legal heirs and sometimes even use the two terms interchangeably, but they are not the same. The confusion usually arises because, in some cases, the nominee and the legal heir may be the same person. In reality, the concepts are very different.

A nominee is essentially the custodian of assets who ensures that the property is smoothly transferred to the rightful successors of the deceased. The nominee does not automatically become the legal heir. Their role is to act as a trustee who receives the assets on behalf of the legal heirs. On the other hand, legal heirs are entitled to inherit not only the assets but also any liabilities attached to them, such as pending taxes, outstanding debts or the need to obtain succession certificates.

In some specific cases, such as EPF or LIC policies, the nominee becomes the direct beneficiary and the benefits are paid out to them. However, in the absence of a nominee, assets are distributed according to personal laws and succession rules such as the Indian Succession Act. In such situations, the process often becomes time-consuming and costly.

It is important to note that a nominee does not have ownership rights over the asset. Their responsibility is limited to ensuring its transfer to the legal heirs. If the legal heirs suspect mismanagement or foul play by the nominee, they have the right to approach the courts for redressal.

Nominee	Legal Heir
Temporary custodian	Actual inheritor
No ownership rights	Inherits assets & liabilities
Ensures smooth transfer	Must settle debts/taxes

Exceptions: In EPF and insurance policies, the nominee is often the beneficiary.

3. MINOR INHERITANCE / TRANSFEREE

When a minor inherits a property, they do not have the legal capacity to manage or sell it. In such situations, the responsibility lies with a natural guardian, usually the parents or a court-appointed guardian. The guardian manages the property until the minor attains the age of 18 years. Any transaction involving the inherited property of a minor, such as a sale, lease or mortgage, requires prior approval of the court to ensure the protection of the minor's financial interests.

Legal Procedures in Minor Inheritance / Transferee

1. Appointment of Guardian – A natural guardian (usually parents) manages the property. If not available, the court appoints a legal guardian under the Guardians and Wards Act, 1890.
2. Court Approval for Transactions – Any sale, lease or mortgage of the minor's property requires prior court permission to prevent misuse.
3. Trust Creation – In some cases, property may be held in trust until the minor reaches eighteen years. Trustees act in the minor's best interest.
4. Income and Benefit Utilization – Any income from the property (like rent or interest) can only be used for the minor's welfare, education and upbringing.
5. Transfer on Attaining Majority – At 18 years, full rights are

transferred to the minor, who can then manage, sell or utilize the property.

4. INTESTATE SUCCESSION

If a person dies without leaving a valid Will, their assets are distributed according to personal succession laws. For Hindus, Jains, Buddhists and Sikhs, the Hindu Succession Act, 1956, applies, whereas Muslims are governed by their laws and Christians and Parsis are covered by the Indian Succession Act, 1925. This process, known as intestate succession, often involves detailed legal procedures and may delay the distribution of property among heirs.

Legal Procedures in Intestate Succession

Here are the main procedures involved:

6. Legal Heir Certificate or Succession Certificate – Heirs must obtain these from the court or local authority to prove their claim.
7. Identification of Class of Heirs – For Hindus, heirs are divided into Class I, Class II, etc., under the Hindu Succession Act, 1956. For Muslims, distribution follows personal Sharia law.
8. Court Proceedings (if disputes arise) – If heirs contest property rights, civil courts intervene to settle claims.
9. Mutation of Property Records – Once legal heirs are confirmed, property records (land, house, etc.) must be updated in the name of the heirs with municipal or revenue authorities.
10. Tax and Debt Settlement – Before distribution, any pending taxes, loans or liabilities of the deceased must be cleared.

5.GUARDIANSHIP IN PROPERTY TRANSFER

Guardianship becomes particularly important in cases where minors or persons with disabilities are involved. A guardian acts as a custodian of the assets and is responsible for maintaining them in the best interests of the heir. However, a guardian cannot misuse or transfer such property for personal benefit. Court approval is necessary before undertaking any transaction that may affect the minor's or dependent's inherited property, ensuring their rights are safeguarded.

So, pointwise:

- A guardian manages a minor's inherited property until age 18 (or 21 if court-appointed).
- Natural guardians (parents) cannot sell, gift, lease or mortgage immovable property without court approval.
- If no natural guardian is available, the court appoints one under the Guardians and Wards Act, 1890.
- To transfer property, the guardian must apply to the court with valuation details and reasons showing benefit to the minor.
- Sale proceeds are usually deposited or reinvested safely and the guardian must provide accounts to the court.
- Upon attaining majority, the minor gets rights and the guardian transfers the property and accounts.

6. SUCCESSION CERTIFICATE (COURT-AUTHORIZED INHERITANCE PROOF)

A succession certificate is issued by a civil court to validate the legal heir(s) of a deceased person who died without a Will. It authorizes the heir to claim debts, securities and other assets.

Process to Obtain a Succession Certificate

11. File a petition in the district court where the deceased last resided.
12. Submit required documents (death certificate, proof of relationship).
13. Court verification and hearing (six to twelve months' processing time).
14. Certificate issuance, enabling asset transfer.

Purpose and Limitations

- Protects debtors making payments in good faith.
- Allows collection of dividends/interest on inherited securities.
- Time-consuming and requires family cooperation.

Alternative Documents

- Legal heir certificate (simpler but less comprehensive).
- Nomination details (for financial assets).

7. POWER OF ATTORNEY (DELEGATING FINANCIAL/LEGAL AUTHORITY)

A PoA is a legal document authorizing someone (an 'agent') to act on behalf of another (the 'principal').

Types of Power of Attorney

- **General PoA** – Broad authority (e.g., managing all financial matters).
- **Special (Limited) PoA** – Specific tasks (e.g., selling a property).

Common Uses

- Managing bank transactions.
- Buying/selling real estate.
- Handling investments in the principal's absence.

Note: A PoA becomes void upon the principal's death.

8. POST-DEATH ASSET TRANSFER PROCESS

After an individual's demise, legal heirs must:

1. Submit the death certificate + legal heir certificate to banks, insurers, etc.
2. If a Will exists, assets are distributed as per its terms.
3. Without a Will, succession laws determine inheritance.
4. Nominees facilitate interim custody until legal heirs claim assets.

Key Challenges

- Disputes among heirs (if no Will exists)
- Delays in court procedures (for succession certificates)
- Tax and debt liabilities on inherited assets

Also from Hachette Reference ...

Chambers

English Vocabulary

- Higher studies • Creative writing • TOEFL/IELTS
- Job interviews • Test prep • Everyday situations
- Office communication

Amazing Rituals of INDIA

Swayam Ganguly

Chambers

BOOK OF INDIAN ELECTION FACTS

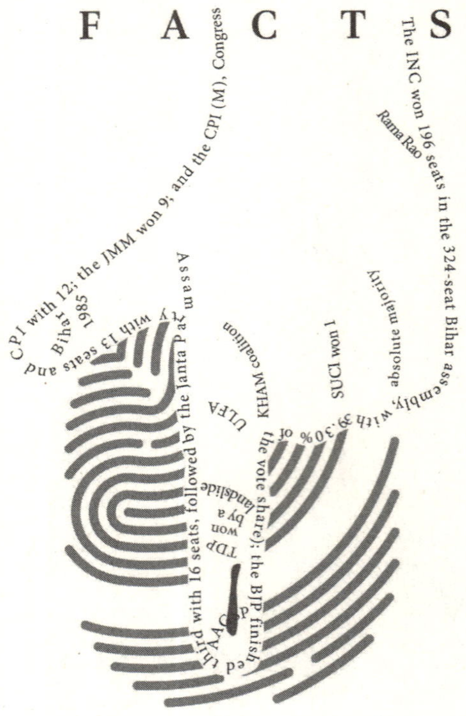

KINGSHUK CHATTERJEE

SURBEK BISWAS

Over 1,000 essential facts

and many non-essential but fascinating ones.

qc

Quick and Concise

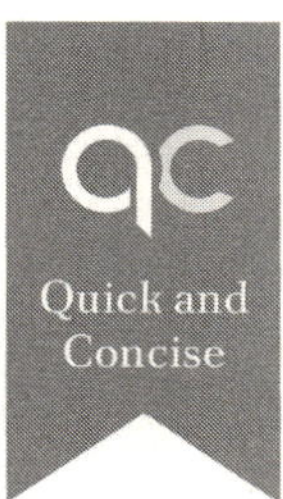

PHILOSOPHY

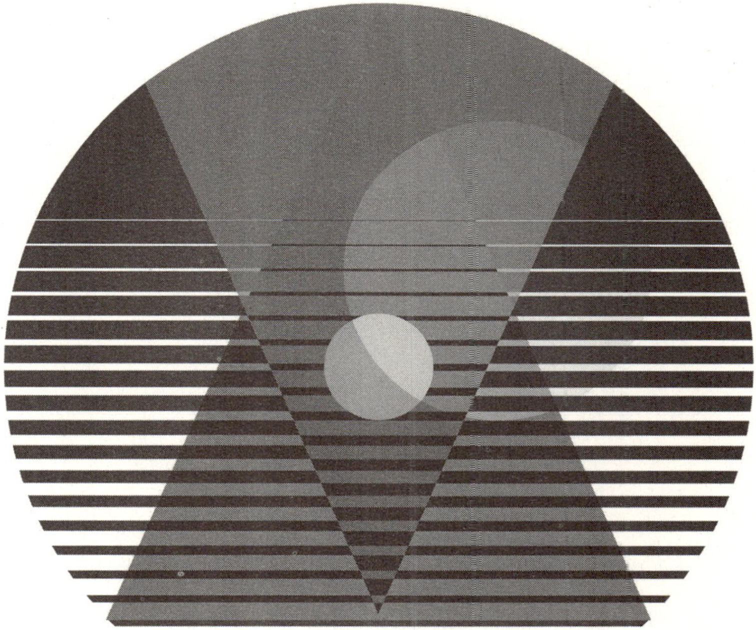

Shamik Chakravarty

H

SELECTED ESSAYS ON THE GITA

Sri Aurobindo

Chambers

General Knowledge Companion

THE MUST-KNOW MANUAL

Indian DEFENCE & SECURITY Handbook